LAMAR'S GAMBLE

LAMAR'S GAMBLE

A TALE OF THE AFL-NFL MERGER

BILLY O'CONNOR AND **FRANK PACE**

Acclaim Press
MORLEY, MISSOURI

Acclaim Press
— Your Next Great Book —

P.O. Box 238
Morley, MO 63767
(573) 472-9800
www.acclaimpress.com

Editor: Randy Baumgardner
Book & Cover Design: Rodney Atchley

Library of Congress Control Number: 2020947667
ISBN: 978-1-948901-76-5 / 1-948901-76-5

First Printing 2021
Printed in the United States of America
10 9 8 7 6 5 4 3 2 1

This publication was produced using available information.
The publisher regrets it cannot assume responsibility for errors or omissions.

To the 343 of my fallen brothers who gave the ultimate sacrifice on 9/11.
To the more than 1,400 rescue workers who have since died and
to the thousands more still battling life-threatening injuries.
To my family, to Alcoholics Anonymous, and to all teachers everywhere.
I'll never forget.

— Billy O'Connor

For my brothers, Bruce and Douglas.

— Frank Pace

ACKNOWLEDGMENTS

Wikipedia defines FACTION as a newly coined literary term describing a text that is based on historical figures, and actual events, woven together with fictitious allegations. Faction is a common term used in European literature.

Most of this book is documented. Some of it is fiction. Obviously we could not be privy to bedroom or boardroom conversations. Thus, it is faction, with the predominant text being FACTUAL.

The events portrayed here are not intended to cause malice, harm, or embarrassment. The authors have retold them in a way to evoke the feeling and meaning of what was said in the context of the time it was said. Additionally, the authors only suggest that the final score of the 1957 Colts-Giants game might have been manipulated to beat the point spread. That actual statement is attributed to a third party, which can be easily verified. The same could be said for the outcome of Super Bowl III. The New York Jets won that game fairly on the field, yet questions still exist. We simply suggest the "what ifs?".

The authors would like to acknowledge our agent, Julia Lord of Lord Literary Management in New York City. Also, Shirley Rash who edited the final manuscript. The authors would also like to thank Armen Keteyian, Dwight Hicks, and Johnny Clams, who wrote the back cover testimonials.

Thanks as well go to Douglas Sikes, Randy Baumgardner and everyone at Acclaim Press, without whom this book could not have happened. Thanks to Jennifer O'Connor for working with two dinosaurs to bring their computer skills into the twenty-first century. To Tom and Cathy Brock for their advice and editing diligence. To Karen Pace, Charlie, Erin and Frankie Moore (plus any little brothers or sisters to come) for their love and support.

Last and not least, to all the people we have met along the way, for the role they have played in helping to make this project a reality.

LAMAR'S GAMBLE

A TALE OF THE AFL-NFL MERGER

"Chiefs batter 49ers to capture Super Bowl LIV."
Good stories seldom start at the beginning.
This one does….

CHAPTER ONE

Overlooking a private lake in South Texas, a manor with the pastoral elegance of Washington's Mount Vernon estate dominated a knoll and demanded attention. The two-story mansion was long and white with a wide marble porch overlooking a screened clay tennis court. Citrus trees and camellias bloomed in the side yard under a storybook gazebo.

Shortly after Christmas 1958, Lamar Hunt plastered himself to an overstuffed armchair and read the back page of the *Dallas Observer* —"Colts Favored to Boot Giants." The shy young man pivoted his eyes from the headline and fastened his thick spectacles back to the television screen. The brittle bow-tied nerd slipped out of his plush loveseat and slid onto a Persian rug. The twenty-six-year-old reached for a yellow pad and began to scribble. Lamar's childhood playmates had nicknamed him "Games" because of his obsession with statistics, sports, and competition. Lamar liked the tag almost as much as he loved the games themselves.

Lamar was rich, really rich, but he wasn't like many wealthy people who feel they're different from the rest of us, the ones who come into the world with an inflated idea of their relationship to it. Lamar was a conservative yet tenacious man searching to get out from under the stigma of his father's shadow. H.L. Hunt was the world's richest man, and nobody would ever let Lamar forget it.

His daddy assumed that Lamar would use his geology degree to work for the family oil business, but big oil was hardly a game. Even if it were, it wouldn't have been Lamar's.

The oil industry was as dirty as its product, and Lamar was Christian, the hard, harsh kind. Morality meant more to him than money. Although it would be hard breaking the news to his overbearing father, Lamar would never be an oilman.

All of that could wait. Today was the National Football League's championship game, and Lamar's beloved Colts were playing. His eyes stayed glued to the screen, ever scribbling on his yellow pad.

—m—

Far from that Texas mansion, three other men were anticipating that championship game. Inside the top-floor bedroom of a five-story Bronx tenement, the trio wore sweaters and appeared to be in their mid-twenties. Feverishly answering four phones equally spaced on a long table, they scribbled on piles of betting slips. A blackboard above them read "Colts 3 1/2 over the Giants."

A husky man with a crew cut growled into a phone, "Okay, Mike, for the Marshall, here's your repeat," Red said. "You've got the Colts minus 3 1/2, twenty times. That's $100 on the Colts."

The second man, shorter and skinnier, squinted before yapping into the phone he was holding. "You've got the Colts minus 3 1/2 for $300," Blinky said. "Glenn, wait. Don't hang up. Wait for your repeat. Glenn for Blinky, you've got the Colts minus 3 1/2, sixty times."

—m—

The third man stood in front of the long Formica table and marked thin chalk lines on the board with every call. Each vertical mark represented a $1,000. When the lines totaled five, Mars crossed them with a horizontal mark.

"We've got twenty grand more on the Colts, but if we move the line to 4, we could get sided," Mars said. "We better keep the line at 3 1/2 for a while."

"Getting sided would be bad enough," Blinky said. "But God forbid we have to go to 4 1/2. We could get middled. That would be disastrous."

"We can't go to 4 1/2," Red said. "That's Bookmaking 101. Ya never let the suckers win both sides of a game. We'll have to eat it. Those gangsters in Vegas are too sharp with these numbers. You watch. The final score will fall somewhere around the spread. The wise guys should run the Treasury. These shysters are always on the money."

—⚬—

A few miles south of that Bronx bookmaking office, anxious fans clad in ties, fedoras, and overcoats filled New York's Yankee Stadium for the 1958 title game. Cigarettes or cigars hung from anxious lips, cheeks denting and puffing with anticipation.

In crowded smoke-filled bars throughout America, customer's eyes fastened to tiny twenty-one-inch, black-and-white screens embedded in massive mahogany cabinets.

In Los Angeles, professional golf hustler Al Besselink, who once finished third in the Masters, settled in after eighteen holes to watch the game's final minute with NFL quarterback John Brodie.

Two overcoat-clad commentators, Chris Schenkel and Chuck Thompson, wore leather gloves and scarves as they called the game's finish. Cold fog blew from Thompson's mouth into the microphone. "Seven seconds to go, the Giants are holding onto a three-point lead. Colts ball, fourth down. Steve Myra and the field goal unit are on the field. If this kick is good, we'll have a tie championship game for the first time in NFL history, Chris."

"Here's the snap, the kick. It's up. It's good. The Colts have tied the game at 17 as time expires." Chuck paused and turned. "Wait a minute. What happens now, Chris? How does this play out?"

"I'm not sure, Chuck. The officials are deliberating now. Up until today, if an NFL game ended in a tie, that was it. Nobody won. I'm as puzzled as you are. While we're waiting, Chris, let's have a word from our sponsor."

After the short commercial, the camera faded from Chuck and zoomed in on Chris.

"Well, during the break, Chuck, our producer told me that we'll have a three-minute pause, a coin toss, and then the first team that scores will win, sudden death if you will. If they win the flip, this favors the Colts. They have momentum and football's greatest quarterback with Unitas."

"We will have to wait and see, Chris. I'm as excited as the fans. One thing's certain. Everyone in those seats today, and everybody at home, has seen one doozy of a battle. Whatta game."

—m—

Ten minutes later, 40 million people remained fixated on Schenkel's voice. "Well, just to recap the overtime so far, Chuck. The Colts lost the toss, but their defense held Giants veteran quarterback Charlie Conerly to three and out. After the punt, the Colts offense put together two first downs, and now Johnny Unitas wants more. He takes the snap. He's back to pass. Unitas has time and completes a long pass to a wide-open Raymond Berry."

The broadcaster's cold breath cast a fog over the microphone.

"Well, that play has the Giants in big trouble, Chris. Unitas has coolly shredded their vaulted defense. They are deep in Giants territory and knocking at the door. Baltimore has a first and goal at the Giants 8 yard line. Remember, the first score of any kind wins the game, so I wouldn't expect the Colts to take any chances."

—m—

Watching in L.A., Brodie said, "They'll kick a field goal and win."

"They ain't kicking a field goal," Besselink said. "Watch and learn what this game is really all about."

—m—

As Chuck continued to broadcast the play-by-play, the television cameras closed in on a playing surface reduced to dust after a long season of use.

"Here we go folks, first and goal from the eight. Here's the snap, a handoff to Ameche up the middle. He's not going anywhere, Chris. Sam Huff stuffs him for a one-yard gain. These last seven yards won't be easy, Chris. Not against a Giants defense that last week held Cleveland's punishing and powerful fullback Jim Brown to just eight yards rushing on this very same field. This amazing Giants defense received the game ball for that 10–0 divisional title game win."

—∞—

Television screens across the country suddenly went blank. Confused face turned to confused face. Viewers at home assumed something was wrong with their sets. A man wearing long johns in his Maryland living room held a cigar in one hand while his other hand smacked the top of a rabbit-eared TV.

—∞—

In L.A, Brodie was confused, too, but for a different reason.

"Why don't they just kick a field goal?"

"I'll tell you why," Besselink said. "Carroll Rosenbloom, my buddy Mike McLaney, and that Canadian chiseler Lou Chesler bet $1 million on the game, but they can't win by a field goal. The line is 3 1/2. They need a touchdown to win their bet."

"Holy shit, $1 million?" Brodie said. "The winner's share is only $4,700. How the hell do you know this?"

"Because if the Colts cover the spread, McLaney offered me $20,000 to pick up part of their winnings. I'm playing in the New Orleans Open next week, and they've laid off the bet with different bookies all over the country."

—∞—

The broadcast resumed, finding the two sportscasters clapping their arms around their shoulders in a futile attempt at comfort.

"Sorry about that technical difficulty," Chuck said. "Someone apparently kicked a cable. Fortunately, the officials called time-out, so none of our viewers missed any action."

—␣␣—

The officials' time-out wasn't actually long enough for NBC to correct their technical difficulties. Whether calculated or by chance, toward the end of the delay, a delirious fan raced onto the field and sailed eighty yards toward the Baltimore huddle. By the time the police corralled him, NBC was able to correct their problem. Rumors still persist that the league had refused to delay the game, consequently, an NBC employee was ordered to race onto the field.

—␣␣—

"Well, back to the play-by-play," Chris said. "Second and goal from the eight folks, here's the snap. Unitas fakes to Ameche. Holy mackerel, he's back to pass…. The Colts quarterback throws and hits Mutscheller in the flats. Mutscheller cuts to the six, to the four, and finally knocked out of bounds at the 1 yard line, stopping the clock. Can you believe that, Chuck? I wasn't expecting that, and neither was the Giants defense…. Risky taking a chance on a pass down there, but it worked. That pass sets the Colts up with a third and goal from the one."

"What a game this packed house has seen here today, Chris. No matter what happens on this play, no one will leave disappointed. This sold-out Yankee Stadium is on its feet…. Can the Giants make a goal-line stand?"

"Here's the snap, Unitas hands off to Ameche, TOUCHDOWN COLTS, TOUCHDOWN COLTS. The Baltimore Colts win the first sudden death game in football history. What an amazing ending to this unforgettable game. The final score Colts 23, Giants 17. What a game, Chuck. What … a … game. Don't go away, folks. After a commercial break, we will be back to recap this epic clash."

—∽∽—

In Los Angeles, Brodie turned. His head jolted sideways, and his eyebrow raised in newfound respect for Besselink's Mob connections.

—∽∽—

A mesmerized twenty-six-year-old Lamar Hunt watched on TV as players in various stages of undress drenched their teammates with champagne. A reporter interviewed the game's star, Johnny Unitas. "Johnny, weren't you afraid that pass on the 8 yard line would get intercepted?"

"Weeb never sent the field goal team in, so my job was to go for the touchdown."

The reporter turned the microphone toward the Colts coach and asked the fifty-one-year-old Ewbank the same question.

"First of all, you don't kick field goals on second or third down. To be successful at anything, you have to take chances. To win, you have to gamble. That's what football is all about—going for it at all costs."

That comment buried itself in Lamar's subconscious, but he was unaware that the seemingly innocuous statement would alter his life in a way that the young statistics nerd could never have imagined.

CHAPTER TWO

Nine years before that remarkable game, the Vegas Strip was alive with the names of the top entertainers of the time. Flashing neon marquees promised performances by Frank Sinatra, Peggy Lee, and Jackie Gleason. In the Sands parking lot, a young Vegas chorus girl satisfied an overweight man in a black Cadillac. Head tilted backwards, the man smiled and groaned.

As Georgia bobbed her head—rhythmically, methodically, yet ever dispassionately—the Caddy's radio blasted Peggy Lee's "Mañana." The enthusiastic, portly man reclined in the driver's seat and grinned. "That's it, baby. Go to town on it. Jesus Christ, you do it, baby, oh baby. That's it. You got it. That's it, aaahhhhh." His screams morphed into a series of jarring laughs before finally descending into a low, recurring moan.

Georgia raised her smiling face. "A screamer, holy shit…. If anyone around here heard you, they would have thought I was killing you."

Her straight hair hung heavily down to her shoulders, where it curled softly inwards. It was the palest ash blonde and shone almost silver under the distant, flashing neon lights.

"Jesus, what a magician," Lou said. "Where the hell did you learn to perform like that? Sorry about the screams. Did they bother you?"

"No, the screams didn't bother me," she said. "On the contrary, I find them gratifying. It's nice to be appreciated."

"That was the best $50 I ever spent. You're one beautiful woman. Do you have a card or something?"

"No. I'm not a streetwalker. I never freelance. When you told me at the bar that your wife was asleep upstairs, I figured why not pick up a few extra bucks. I usually work strictly through the agency."

As she left the car, her purple high heels stabilized two shapely, nyloned legs, which rose to a short white leather skirt that barely covered her perfectly pear-shaped ass. The cheap yet classy Georgia sashayed to the driver's side of the car and leaned on the Caddy's open window. She scribbled her number and handed it to the satisfied customer.

"Ah, what the hell…. Look, next time you're in town, forget the agency. Call me at home. My name's Georgia, like the state. I cost a bit more, but I'm worth it." She winked.

CHAPTER THREE

C arroll Rosenbloom, "C.R." as he was known to friends, was all things to all people. He was complex, brilliant, and ruthless, especially in business and finance.

A gambler by nature, he purchased the Baltimore Colts for $13,000 in 1953 and, fewer than two decades later, traded the franchise for the Los Angeles Rams for an estimated $20 million. Like many powerful men, if you crossed him once, he could be endlessly vindictive. To him, life was a contact sport.

—⁓—

When Carroll lurched into the Colts conference room that in- credible Monday morning, Cleveland Browns owner Art Modell was telling an anecdote, "For two weeks, this putz calls up one of my offices. Every night he gets the NBA line and bets three or four games. I swear to God. He loses twenty-four straight games. The following week, he calls again looking for the NBA lines. My clerk tells him, 'we don't have the NBA tonight. It's the All-Star break. How about hockey?' He says, 'Hockey? What the fuck do I know about hockey?'"

Modell laid his hands on his knees and cackled. "Ya believe this schmuck? Ya can't make this shit up. What does he know about hockey? What does he know about anything? I'm surprised no one has to water this asshole twice a day."

After the predictable laughs, Modell grinned at Rosenbloom and widened his eyes.

"Our league's no longer just filler between baseball seasons, Carroll. The networks finally realize that pro football is great theater. That championship game galvanized America. Imagine ... sudden death on national television in front of 45 million people...."

Modell was middle-aged, thick across the waist, and wore a brown tie. His black hair was prudently pushed across a partially bald head.

"Modell's right," Rams executive Tex Schramm said. "We couldn't have written a better script. Unitas and Raymond Berry shook the nation by its throat Sunday. The newspapers are calling it the greatest game ever played."

"A wonderful day for us with brilliant press." Art Rooney was pockmarked, double-chinned, with a short neck and a fat face. "But anyone with a banshee's sense still wouldn't buy a football team."

"Oh? You'd be surprised, Art. I've heard quite a few people are looking for franchises." Rosenbloom usually spoke in a soft, slow, measured twang that only thinly disguised his inner steel. "Well, to hell with that. Let's keep this club exclusive. With this new television revenue, if we minimize expenses, we might finally turn a profit."

In 1933, Carroll, the son of a Russian Jewish immigrant, had taken over a small Virginia factory that his father wanted liquidated. For the next seven years, Carroll's government connections steered Blue Ridge Overalls through a series of denim clothes contracts with the US Civilian Conservation Corps.

He built Blue Ridge into a 7,000-employee conglomerate, earning Carroll the title "America's Overalls King." He sold his interests for immeasurable wealth and $20 million in stock the year of that overtime game, enabling him to further diversify his interests. He acquired several companies, including Seven Arts Productions, which backed numerous movies and Broadway plays, such as *Funny Girl*.

Carroll's eyes narrowed with concern as he turned to Tex Schramm.

"Tex, what do you know about this guy, Lamar Hunt? He's from your neck of the woods."

"Shit, everybody in Texas either knows or does business with the Hunts," Schramm said. "As for Lamar, he's the kind of guy that you'd overlook in a crowd of two. He speaks like a frightened child in catechism class, but just because he looks like a high school civics teacher, don't underestimate him. There's nothing dull about his mind, and shoot, ya always gotta remember that his daddy's the richest man in America."

CHAPTER FOUR

On a clear spring day, Lamar's doting wife fidgeted with his tie. Rosemary was a handsome woman, small, lithe, and tidy in blue slacks and a sweater.

"How do you expect to make a good impression with that silly, old brown bow tie, Lamar?"

"My tie won't make any difference in Chicago, Sugar. Either Wolfner sells me the Cardinals or he doesn't."

"That may be so, but I'm your wife. I won't have you running around like a ragamuffin. Can't you forget about football for a few minutes … at least long enough to say a proper goodbye? You know that Lamar Junior is devastated that you won't be here for his first Little League game. I hope you're doing the right thing buying this team."

"Sugar, you know my family comes first, but this time Lamar will just have to understand. You know my dream has always been to bring a professional football team to Dallas. This is my chance. If Wolfner sells me the Cardinals, I'll move them to Texas."

He glided his hands up and down his sport coat and tapped his pants pockets in a last-minute search before having a second thought.

"Did you pack my Bible?"

"Don't worry. I checked for your Bible before I checked for your plane ticket. Even though you know I don't agree with you, I hope you get what you're after. One way or another, it seems like you Hunts always do."

—w—

Later that afternoon, both men sat on a leather sofa in the Cardinals office. Walter Wolfner's suit appeared to have leaped from *Gentleman's Quarterly* while Hunt's screamed simplicity.

"Tell the Bidwells I won't even consider 49 percent," Lamar said. "I need controlling interest. The Cardinals will never make money in Chicago. Let's face it. This town belongs to George Halas and the Bears. The Bidwells need money, and I need a team to move to Dallas. Let's do some business."

"Are you crazy? Dallas?" Wolfner said. "You want to move the Cardinals to Dallas? That's the last place our league wants to go. Dallas had an NFL team three years ago. They drew more people on the road than at home. Carroll Rosenbloom had to move them to Baltimore to survive. Pro football doesn't sell in the South, never will. The South belongs to college football."

"Then sell me 100 percent. Make it my problem."

"The other owners will never approve the sale. Their profit margin is too thin already, and just the cost of flying teams to Dallas would double their overhead. No, I'm sorry. They've stressed repeatedly, no expansion."

"Then how can we do business?" Lamar asked.

"If it were my team, I'd sell the whole shooting match. You're not the only one looking to buy the Cardinals. Others have expressed interest. In the past months, the Bidwells have had offers from Bud Adams in Houston, Billy Sullivan in Boston, Max Winter in Minneapolis, and Bob Howsam in Denver, but the Bidwells insist on retaining controlling interest. Take the 49 percent."

"No. I have to have the controlling interest. My daddy always says, 'Partners are only good for dancing.' I hate to say it, but it looks like we wasted each other's time. I might as well head back to Texas.'"

—⁓—

Despite available seats in first class, Lamar squeezed between two women in coach. Airborne twenty minutes, a stewardess paused at Lamar's aisle and said to the golden-haired lady by the window, "Would you like a cocktail, madam?"

"Yes, a screwdriver," she said. "Please make it strong. Flying scares me half to death."

The stewardess served her an iced orange juice and placed a small bottle of vodka next to it on her tray. She turned to Lamar. "Would you like a cocktail, sir?"

Scribbling on his ever-present pad, Lamar didn't even look up.

"No. Not right now," he murmured.

The stewardess turned to the larger lady on the aisle. "Cocktail, madam?"

"No, thank you," she said.

The thin blonde lady in the window seat looked out at the twilight dying in the west. The green glow it left on the rippling water below turned it the color of jade. Her stomach tightening, she held up her plastic cup. "Stewardess, this drink's not strong enough."

"I'm sorry, madam. The bottles are measured. We're not permitted to let you make your own."

Lamar ignored his pad a moment and looked at the stewardess like she had just told him he was about to be pushed out of the doorway of the aircraft.

"Wait. What did you say?" Lamar raised his voice. "Young lady, did you say, 'Make your own?'"

The surprised stewardess started to stammer until Lamar interrupted.

"No, sorry, nothing. Never mind. Please, ignore what I just said."

Lamar snatched a pen from his pocket and scribbled the names Wolfner had mentioned in one column: Bud Adams, Billy Sullivan, Bob Howsam, and Max Winter. Under those names, he penned his own, Lamar Hunt. Adjoining the first column, he jotted the cities that the men represented: Houston, Boston, Denver, Minnesota, and Hunt's own Dallas. Upon reflection, he then penciled in New York and Los Angeles with question marks alongside them.

His demeanor changed from a man who knew he might do something to a man who knew that he would. He radiated a sly smile, shoved the pen back into his coat pocket, and signaled the stewardess.

"Excuse me, my dear. Bring me a Jack Daniels Black on the rocks with a water back ... if it's not too much trouble.?"

When she served him the drink, Lamar asked the stewardess for some stationary. He had a long-honed habit of taking copious notes on whatever paper was available. Many of his brainstorms had been sketched out on the backs of envelopes or in the margins of magazines and newspapers. For this stroke of inspiration, he knew that he needed more. So meticulous was Lamar that by the time the American Airlines flight landed in Dallas, he had sketched out the plans for his new league.

In short, neat, penmanship he had outlined provisions for the prospective owners, the rough estimates of the cost of equipment, and the needed revenue from ticket sales. He went so far as to draw up a rough schedule for the first season, including the likely weekends that the regular season would begin and end. He folded the three sheets of onion skin writing paper into his ever-present yellow pad and sat supremely satisfied.

Lamar couldn't have been more content unless he was witnessing what was happening at that very moment in his hometown. With two out in the sixth inning and a man on second, Lamar's son delivered a clean single up the middle to win the game. Rosemary beamed, but Lamar Jr.'s accomplishment that cool spring night was pyrrhic. Just like Lamar Sr.'s relationship with his own father, one approving smile from his dad would have meant more to Lamar Jr. than all the winning hits in the world.

—⟋⟋⟍—

Later that evening, Lamar Jr. sat yoga-style on his bed, pounding a baseball into the mitt covering his left hand. Sitting next to his disappointed son, Lamar tried to have a heart to heart.

"Your Mom told me about your winning hit. I wish I could have been there. I'll try never to miss another game, promise. Let me tell you what my daddy never told me…. I'm proud of you … awfully proud. But I need you to be proud of me too. Before that can happen, I have to be proud of myself."

"I know you're working hard, Dad." Lamar Jr. wrapped the glove around the ball, tossed it aside, and gave his father a grave gaze. "You don't have to work as hard as you work. We have plenty of money. We're not normal people. We're Hunts."

"That's an awful thing to say. Just because we're Hunts, it doesn't mean we're entitled to anything. Never forget that your grandfather accomplished everything through hard work and by refusing to quit. A lot of his character rubbed off on us. Be proud of that work ethic and of him."

CHAPTER FIVE

Lamar sat at a small, gray, metal desk, wearing a modest gray suit and bow tie. The desk and outfit matched his gray spectacles, which accentuated his gray-hazel eyes, but Tex Schramm was dead-on. Not a drop of gray clouded Hunt's manic mind.

"Bud Adams, please. Tell him that if it's not too much trouble, Lamar Hunt would like a word with him." Lamar whistled and tapped a pencil on his desk while awaiting Adams. "Bud Adams? Lamar Hunt here. Can you spare a few minutes? I hope I'm not bothering you, but a little birdy told me that you recently tried to buy the Chicago Cardinals and move them to Houston."

The man Lamar was seeking to invest in his new league was his total opposite. The flamboyant Adams was jokingly known in Houston as "the rich Texan who bought his dog a boy." In those early days, Lamar was unnervingly shy, almost apologetic about his very appearance, which had earned him the nickname "Mister Peepers," after a popular television show of the day.

The diffident Lamar jotted short notes on his ever-present pad while he listened to Adams.

"Yeah, I had the same problem, Bud. Those damn Yankees don't want us Southern boys to play in their league. They'd prefer to take their football and go home. But I have a rather radical idea. Suppose we started our own league, a Southern league. Does that proposition interest you?"

If Adams's basement office were any smaller, it could have been a movie theater. Alongside the indoor lily pond sat a huge barbeque pit. His desk looked like a flight pad. The formidable and ostentatious Bud Adams wore a floor-length white leather coat and a black Stetson.

"Our own league, huh?" Adams said. "Not just yeah but hell yeah. Goddammit, Hunt. You've made my day. I think you're onto something here. Glad you caught me. I was just on my way out."

"Bucking the old guard won't be easy," Lamar said. "But if you're interested, I reckon we can pull this off."

"Imagine that? Our own league? I'm chomping at the bit just thinking about it," Adams said. "Those NFL boys fed me some bullshit about expansion watering down talent. With you in Houston and me in Dallas, can you imagine the rivalry? Giants-Cleveland or Packers-Bears couldn't compare to an all-Texas shootout."

"That's my way of thinking too," Lamar said. "Well, Bud, let me get back to you. I'll make a few calls. I can't promise anything, but I'll update you when I know where this is going."

Lamar cradled the handset and immediately lifted it again, "Billy Sullivan, please, tell him, Lamar Hunt from Dallas…."

CHAPTER SIX

The ocean that night was black as coal and smooth as a baby's bottom, the moon peeking out from lustrous silver clouds. Soft, rolling waves welled over the rocks of the Miami shoreline.

In a suite twenty-two floors above the ecosystem, a wide man wore a blue robe and green slippers. Lou Chesler was a Canadian "entrepreneur" who, within five years, would be instrumental in bringing gambling to the Bahamas. Over 300 pounds with a fondness for urinating outdoors, Chesler was nicknamed "Moose" by his friends. When Chesler needed advice on staffing the Monte Carlo Casino in Freeport, he would turn to Meyer Lansky, the reputed controller of gambling in the Caribbean. Along with Bugsy Siegel, Lansky had co-founded the old Murder Incorporated gang.

Chesler was yet another close friend of Carroll Rosenbloom, and the two had numerous business dealings. Sometimes he traveled with the Colts, and his son even visited their training camp. Rosenbloom had invited Moose to a fundraiser that weekend, and he needed a date. Recalling that the exquisite prostitute he had met years ago in Vegas now lived in Miami, the portly Lou Chesler dialed information and hoped for the best. He rolled a seven.

I don't know if you remember me, but I sure as hell remember you, and I'm in town," Lou said. "Yep, that's right, Georgia, right here in Miami. I'm at the Hilton for four days." He opened the small refrigerator, pulled out a two-ounce bottle of Chivas Regal, and sat it next to the phone. "Come on, Georgia. I know you're married now. I know you're out of the business. It's not about that. I've got a dozen numbers I can call for that. For this gig, I need someone with a brain on my arm, not just eye candy. These are important people. I don't know another woman in this town who can pull this off. Come on, for old times' sake. We'll have a couple of laughs. You might even do yourself some good. It's at Joe Kennedy's house."

Lou smiled into the phone.

"You'll go? Wonderful. I thought the name Kennedy might change your mind. I'll pick you up tomorrow night about 8 p.m."

He cracked the scotch and built a drink.

"Don't pick you up? Meet here at the hotel? Okay, but don't be late. That's right, 8 p.m. By the way, make sure you dress appropriately. It's formal."

—⚏—

On the arm of the avuncular Lou, Georgia observed the party's bustle from the balcony. Statuesque women wearing strapless gowns and dripping jewelry clung to older businessmen wearing black tuxedos. A twenty-piece orchestra played "I've Got You Under My Skin."

"Kennedy lives here? Wow, impressive. You've come a long way since Vegas."

"This is hardly my normal circle of friends," Lou said. "I'm only a friend of a friend. The only reason I'm here is that it's a fundraiser, and Kennedy wants to dip into my wallet. Old man Joe's running his son for the presidency. Because the kid's a war hero, Kennedy thinks he has a chance, but Jack can't win. He's a Roman Catholic."

Looking down at the patio, Georgia scanned the guests slowly, hungrily.

"A smart girl could change her life here."

"Easy, girl. Slow down. You're here to help me. Remember?"

"Don't tell me how to act," Georgia snapped. She composed herself before giving Lou a slight peck on the cheek.

"Don't worry. When the night is over, you'll have no complaints. No man has ever been dissatisfied with Sweet Georgia."

"Why do you think I phoned you?" Lou said. "I know you'll come through."

Georgia nodded at Lou and sipped her champagne before glancing around again at the packed, opulent, highbrow Kennedy mixer. The abundance of diamonds would have made a jewel thief salivate, the gowns from European design houses, the patent leather shoes handmade.

"Only beautiful people get to swim in this pool."

"I knew there'd be plenty of gorgeous women here. Kennedy loves the ladies. Rumor has it his sons are players too."

"And you're not?" Continuing to ogle the guests, she said, "I've never met a powerful man yet who didn't polish his ego with a pretty woman's panties."

Georgia had a tan even in the winter and the smoothest skin Lou had ever seen. When Lou looked into the small lights playing in her narrowed eyes, he saw a salacious look.

"It might be better for both our interests if tonight, at least for a little while, you pretend to be a lady."

"Pretend to be a lady?" She jerked away. "I am a lady."

"Of course you are." He paused. "But being a lady is a lot like being smart. If you have to keep telling people you are, they will begin to have their suspicions. Come on. I'll introduce you to the man who invited me."

Lou's remark garnered another icy stare from Georgia. The pair strolled downstairs past the oil paintings on the wall and entered a glass door leading to the enormous patio, where Joe Kennedy was holding court with three distinguished men.

"Never trust an Irishman with a bottle of booze or a Jew with a box of matches," Kennedy joked.

"I hope I never have to go that route to make a buck," Rosenbloom smiled.

"The first couple of million is the hardest, Carroll." Joe smiled. "After that, you can just fake the next ten."

"If everyone in the country were as big a Colt fan as you, I wouldn't have to fake anything," Carroll said.

"My dad seems more interested in that damn football team than my political career." Jack Kennedy smiled.

Among the four, Rosenbloom stood out. He had a boxer's

build—narrow hips, a boilerplate flat stomach and ax-handle-wide shoulders..He was both dapper and confident.

Rosenbloom grinned and extended his hand to the two new-comers.

"Hello there, Moose. Glad you could make it."

"I wouldn't have missed it for the world, C.R." Chesler nodded toward his date. "Let me introduce you to my dear friend, Georgia."

Carroll was social and friendly enough to his pal, Moose, but his eyes had locked on Georgia. Not wanting to appear lecherous, he paid her a quick compliment before turning back to Chesler.

"Well, Moose. There has never been anything wrong with your eyesight. She's stunning," Carroll said. He nodded back in her direction. "Hello, Georgia, a pleasure to meet you. Let me introduce you and Lou here to our host, Joe Kennedy."

Kennedy extended his right hand.

"Well, hello, Lou. Welcome to our little shack. You said this charming, young creature that you've brought with you is named Georgia?"

She extended her hand.

"That's right, Georgia, like the state. It's a pleasure to meet you, Mr. Kennedy. What a stunning home you have. I've never seen anything quite like it."

"Please, Georgia, call me Joe. You've already met C.R. This is my son Jack and one of my dearest friends, Senator Everett Dirksen."

Georgia recognized the two instantly and quickly grasped the sphere of influence she was in.

Joe Kennedy turned from Georgia.

"As I was saying, gentlemen, the electorate must be controlled. The great unwashed can't be the ones allowed to make the decisions that affect this country's future. Most voters don't understand how Washington works. Their ignorance could put the country at considerable risk. Why, they might even vote against their own interests."

He lowered his voice, looked from man to man, hoisted his drink, and laughed.

"Or even worse, they might vote against ours."

The men grinned and clicked glasses.

"I agree, Joe," Carroll said. "Television is the key to controlling the next election. It reaches right into the electorate's bedrooms. Politics has always been about the latest form of mass media. When photography was in its infancy, Lincoln recognized its importance and grew a beard to soften his appearance. When radio began, FDR recognized its possibilities and initiated his fireside chats. Television is the future, I tell you. It has already changed football. I guarantee that it will be the key to your son's presidential run. But enough business, we're boring this beautiful young lady."

"Bored? On the contrary," Georgia said. "Please, gentlemen, continue. I work part-time in television. I find this conversation fascinating."

"Of course, even with the advent of mass media, one wonders to what extent any politician believes what he says," Dirksen said. "Most, of course, never do. Television will mass deliver the opiate necessary to soothe our electorate. Used properly, it will allow voters the comfort of opinion without the discomfort of thought." Dirksen turned to an approaching Bobby Kennedy, sipped his drink, and smiled. "It's always those pesky sincere voters who muck things up for young politicians like you who want to rise normally."

Bobby flashed his signature grin.

"There's a fellow here tonight named Marshall McLuhan," Joe Kennedy said. "He wrote a book about the media's influence on the masses. His concepts deserve careful study. He proposes that as hearth and fire were once the center of our homes or lairs, now the television set will become the center of modern man's being. All points of the room will converge upon its presence, and the eye will watch it even as the mind will doze. Mark my words. Whoever controls that box will control elections."

Never diffident, Bobby chimed in.

"Andy Warhol said that people will always watch something rather than nothing. Between a plain wall, abstract art, or a flickering commercial, the eyes will always choose whatever's moving."

"Andy Warhol is that artist fellow isn't he, Bobby?"

Bobby nodded.

Joe Kennedy turned to the others. "Bobby's always been more attuned to today's culture than I am. So now, gentlemen, if you will excuse me"—he turned to Georgia—"and lady, of course. I'm being a poor host. Come on, Jack. We need to spread ourselves around a bit. Let's mingle with our guests."

Kennedy and his two sons left and moved toward another group of smiling and adoring cocktail sippers.

Lou turned to Georgia. "Mr. Rosenbloom owns the world-champion Baltimore Colts."

"Guilty as charged," Carroll said. "But if football were my only livelihood, I wouldn't be here tonight, and I wouldn't have had the opportunity to meet your charming companion. What do you do for a living, Georgia?"

"Like you, Mr. Rosenbloom, I have varied interests."

"Call me Carroll, please."

"Like you, Carroll, I have varied interests. I sing, and for the last few years. as I have mentioned, I've done local weather on television. So, you can see why I found your conversation about television's potential power fascinating."

The attraction between Carroll and Georgia was palpable. When their eyes connected, everyone else disappeared. Dirksen excused himself, and after an awkward pause, Lou tried to re-mind Georgia who she came with.

"C'mon, Georgia, we've taken up enough of Mr. Rosenbloom's valuable time."

"Please, Lou, since when do you address me as Mr. Rosenbloom? You always call me C.R. and so should your friend."

He gently grasped Georgia's right hand in a show of affection.

"My time has never been so valuable that it can't be spent chatting with a stunning young lady. I hope I have the pleasure of seeing you again, Georgia."

"Well, we can't control the future, Carroll, but I certainly hope so."

As the two walked away, Georgia turned her face over her left shoulder and looked back at Carroll. The hunger in her eyes made his own eyes shut and his mouth gasp, as though someone had jabbed him in the solar plexus. His cheek creased with the beginning of an introspective smile.

"Be careful of that guy, sweetheart," Lou said. "He's out of your league … generous but ruthless."

"Maybe Rosenbloom's the one who should be careful." Georgia was steel-eyed serious. "I'm not that confused, naïve little girl that you knew in Vegas."

Then as an afterthought, she laughed. "I could do Rosenbloom in five minutes, but I'd make sure to take thirty…. He'd blow like a volcano."

CHAPTER SEVEN

A diverse group of businessmen who would come to be known as "the Foolish Club" met in a Dallas conference room. Amongst the eight, the flamboyant Bud Adams stood out. He wore his floor-length white leather coat with a matching cowboy hat and gave the impression that he was the most important person in the room. In contrast, Lamar's slight build and impeccable manners provided him the valuable asset of making other people feel like they were the most important persons in the room.

"Y'all know each other, if not personally, at least by reputation," Lamar said. "To save time, I'll make a quick pass around the table: Billy Sullivan from Boston, Bud Adams from Houston, Bob Howsam from Denver, Max Winter from Minneapolis, Ralph Wilson from Buffalo, Harry Wismer from New York, and finally, Barron Hilton from L.A. I hope you gentlemen don't mind, but I've asked my dad to sit in; but let me stress that he's not personally involved."

All the men nodded in H.L.'s direction.

"I'm here strictly as a spectator," H.L. said. "I confine my football investments to a few misplaced wagers on the Southeast Conference every Saturday." This garnered the desired smiles, and with the ice broken, Lamar slung his pitch.

"Two years ago, the Yankees ran the Dodgers and Giants out of New York. Fans felt disgusted, betrayed. Although Walter O'Malley's Brooklyn Dodgers were actually making money, Ebbets Field was rickety and small and, in this new age of automobiles, short on parking. They had stars like Gil Hodges, Pee Wee Reese, and Duke Snider and had even broken the baseball color barrier in 1947 with superstar Jackie Robinson. Black stars Roy Campanella and Don Newcombe soon followed.

"They had the marquee names and had finally exorcised their Fall Classic demons by bringing a title back to Brooklyn, but along with his World Series, O'Malley wanted a new stadium.

"For ten years, O'Malley, a man of great vision, haggled with city officials to build the 'Bums' a new home. He wanted a 55,000-seat domed stadium at the corner of Flatbush and Atlantic Avenues complete with a fully automated ticketing system and a movie theater. O'Malley had the financing for the stadium but not for the land.

"But as I said, O'Malley had vision. He went to Robert Moses, the public planning czar and the most powerful man in New York, asking him to condemn the land, making it cheaper to obtain. The trouble was Moses also had a vision, and it was inflexible. He saw driving as the future of New York transportation and envisioned the Dodgers moving out to Flushing Meadows, Queens.

"The land was publicly owned and would create fewer traffic jams than downtown Brooklyn. When the two continually banged heads, O'Malley decided to look west. Los Angeles was a booming city and willing to offer his Dodgers hundreds of acres of downtown land.

"The New York Giants considered moving also. The home of nine pennants and three World Series, the Polo Grounds had been the envy of the entire league, a 55,000-seat cathedral seated squarely amid the glamour of Upper Manhattan. More than 1.5 million fans had packed the Polo Grounds each year at its peak, but by 1957 that number had dropped to just 654,000. Faced with declining revenue and more and more New Yorkers moving to the outer boroughs, city officials looked to claim the land for public housing.

"Horace Stoneham studied the crumbling Polo Grounds, which hadn't been renovated in decades, and feigned interest for a move to Minneapolis, where their AAA franchise was taking up residence. After a series of private meetings, O'Malley convinced him that they could continue their rivalry out in California. Stoneham agreed to move the Giants to San Francisco.

"Those moves were as popular as un-popped pimples, yet now both baseball teams are thriving in new stadiums built on the West Coast. With newly created rivalries, expansion could be more profitable and more successful for football."

Adams interrupted, "Show them the map, Lamar."

Lamar wheeled a map of the United States from the corner of his office while Adams whispered to the men, "Did you see how detailed that explanation was? He thinks a useless statistic doesn't exist. I've never seen anything like it, compulsive really. You boys are getting off easy. He's been bombarding me with numbers for weeks."

Lamar stood in front of the map and circled his pointer around the Northeast.

"The NFL has twelve teams but only two west of the Mississippi and none south of Washington. Their entire demographic is smaller than Texas. Why? Highways, motels, and jet airplanes have shrunk the country. Robert Moses was right but so were Walter O'Malley and Horace Stoneham. This country is expanding. We'll go where the NFL is not and start something new. Of course, the cornerstones of any new league would have to be the coastal cities of New York and Los Angeles, which is why I've invited Barron Hilton and Harry Wismer here."

Hearing his name, Hilton spoke up.

"I'm in the hotel business. I wouldn't know a three-point field goal from a three o'clock checkout time. When Lamar called me, I was reluctant. I don't like to invest outside my field of expertise, but I'm no fool"—he stole a quick glance at H.L.—"I'll listen to anything a Hunt has to say about making money."

"Thanks for the vote of confidence, Barron," Lamar said. "Look, boys. I'm not here to waste anybody's time. I'll be blunt. I want to start a new football league. The buy-in is going to be $100,000, and we'll need $25,000 upfront to set up operations."

Formidable and persuasive, Adams towered over the other potential owners.

"Fellas, Lamar has a great idea here. Last year NFL attendance was so good that this year they have decided to broadcast only their sold-out home games. That'll sell even more tickets. Their league has 3 million fans already. I'm telling you with more teams in more cities, future profits will be limitless. The Southwest will definitely support pro football."

Bob Howsam whipped out his checkbook.

"I know that Denver will support a franchise. Here's my $25,000 in good faith. I'll have the rest within twenty-four hours."

"This has been tried before, Lamar," Minnesota's Max Winter said. "The NFL will protect its product and its pro football monopoly ruthlessly. You better be ready for one hell of a fight."

"Thanks, Max. I expect that, but y'all have my word. I'll never quit."

One of the eight prospective owners was more cautious than the others. As a football guy, Harry Wismer was keenly aware of the risks involved. Risks that would eventually have the men in the room that day refer to themselves as " The Foolish Club."

"I don't know," Wismer said. "The Giants own New York, and I'm far from a wealthy man. It's a dicey proposition." He rubbed his hands through his hair and the corner of his bottom lip turned downward. "I've been a broadcaster for over twenty years with the Lions, Redskins, and Notre Dame. Fighting the Giants in New York? I just don't know."

He thought a minute and finally pounded his fist upon the table.

"You know what? The hell with it. God hates a coward. Count me in."

"That a boy, Harry. I love your style," Max Winter said. "I always enjoyed your broadcasts. Anyone remember that '57 Sugar Bowl?" Winter turned to the others in the room. "When Harry called that game, he got so excited that he said a ball carrier ran across the 50 to the 55 yard line."

"I hear ya," Ralph Wilson said. "Harry announces football games the way holdup victims yell for cops."

"Yeah, well, if this idea of Lamar's turns sour," Harry shot back, "I might have to pull a few hold-ups myself. I'm not as well-healed as the rest of you fellas."

"I'll go along with the others, Hunt," Hilton said. "I'll trust your instincts and ignore mine. I just hope to God that you know football the way your father over there knows oil."

"I know my business all right," H.L. answered. "But anyone with a brain wouldn't underestimate my son, and you gentlemen shouldn't either. He has my full confidence and support."

"So, we're all agreed? Good," Lamar said. "Before we pull the trigger, I'm going to make one more diplomatic plea to the NFL to consider expansion. If that doesn't work, then I believe we're gonna be in business."

"Well, if this scheme comes to fruition, I'm going to have to compete in New York with one of the most revered teams in pro football," Wismer said. "I think I'll call my team the Titans. After all, titans are larger than giants. Might as well let them know upfront that we're not looking to compete. We're looking to be bigger and better."

Back in his office two days later, a broad gold wedding ring on the fourth finger of Lamar's left hand was his only jewelry. That finger silently tapped the surface of his desk. Lamar liked to give bad news to his partners fast and straight. As soon as he had hung up from NFL commissioner Bert Bell, Lamar dialed Bud Adams.

"Bell said that even if the NFL were interested in expansion, Texas would be their last choice," Lamar said. "A new league's our only option, partner."

"This is your show, Lamar," Adams said. "But I was thinking that since you've talked to him, anyway, it might not be a bad idea to offer our league's top job to Bell. We'll double his money. As a former commissioner of the NFL, he would give us instant respectability."

"That might be a pipe dream, Bud, but it can't hurt to make him an offer. Come to think of it when Bert Bell coached the Eagles, Davey O'Brien was his quarterback. Davey works for my father. That might give us an in. I'll have Davey meet with Bell."

Wearing his ever-present white Stetson, Bud Adams stretched his long legs out on a desk so large his snakeskin boots appeared to be adrift in the Pacific.

"Yeah, have Davey meet him and see where it goes. Ya gotta realize one thing, though. If he accepts the job, we're really pissing in their grits." Adams smiled.

"Maybe we should rethink it then?" Lamar said. "I was hoping that despite the competition from our new league, things wouldn't get too vicious."

"You think that they're gonna play nice? Forget it, Lamar. That will never happen. Listen, there's only one twentieth-century organization that I can think of more ruthless than the NFL."

"What organization is that?"

"The Third Reich," Adams said.

Adams heard Hunt snicker through the receiver.

"Don't you dare laugh, Lamar. We're plowing close to their cotton here. These boys will come after us hard. If Bell doesn't take the job, make sure O'Brien tells him to keep his mouth shut about our new league. We don't want to poke a hornet's nest for nothing or have our investors embarrassed before they even sign."

"No. I'm not worried about Bell running his mouth," Lamar said. "I know him well enough to know he won't say anything to anybody. He has always been the consummate professional."

CHAPTER EIGHT

The eastern sun broke high and hot, scorching the state of Texas like a sun lamp. In the front seat of an old Buick, Lamar spun the air conditioner valve to max, half hoping the noise might drown out his father's skepticism.

"You're crazy taking this risk," H.L. said.

"To be successful at anything you have to gamble," Lamar said. "You took risks with your career."

"Come into the oil business with me. You have a geology degree. Use it. There's no money in football, plus you'll be doing business with some unsavory characters."

"If complete strangers have faith in me, why don't you?"

"They have faith in the Hunt name, not you."

"So, that's it? You think they only have faith in my name and not me. Are you worried that I'll fail and disgrace you?

"No. I'm worried that you're not aware of the sacrifices that you'll have to make in order to succeed."

"You mean my family?"

"Son, I'm not one for philosophy, but a man makes two big decisions in life. First, where am I going? Second, who am I taking with me? If he answers the second question before he answers the first, he's in big trouble. I don't believe Rosemary shares your commitment."

"Look who's talking. Your success cost you your family. I won't allow that. In that respect, you're right. My family's much more important to me than yours was to you."

Stung by the remark, his father thought a few moments before attempting amends. He grabbed his son's knee and looked directly into his eyes. "Look, I thought success would be the answer to everything. I was far from perfect. I was selfish and single-minded. I had to be. Someday you'll realize that some things aren't planned. They just happen."

"You made deliberate decisions."

"Damn right I did. I had to commit 120 percent to succeed. You'll have to do that too."

"Other successful men have balanced careers and family," Lamar said.

"The longer you live with your dreams, the more important they become. In the end, you'll sacrifice more than you could ever imagine saving them," H.L. said. "Remember, this is no longer about you. You have investors. If you fail, you can always fall back on the oil business. Many of them don't have that luxury."

"I'm not even thinking about the oil business. It's just not for me. I'll never succeed in a business I hate."

"If you let these men down, what happens to them and their families?"

Lamar said nothing. His dad had hit a nerve, so he just bit his lower lip, turned, and stared out at the monotonous, syncopated, ever-bobbing, oil wells of South Texas.

Later that night, Rosemary unfastened the ties of her terry-cloth robe and turned down the covers on their bed.

"Lamar, I'm worried about this new venture."

"Worried? Worried about what? You think that I'll fail?"

"No. You'll never allow yourself to fail. I'm worried that if you succeed, we're never going to see you."

"You don't have to worry about that. You know nothing's more important to me than my family."

Rosemary slid into bed and shoved her hand beneath his undershirt to snuggle up. "I just have a bad feeling about this. Sometimes I feel that we're forgetting what we once had. Remember when we were the only two people in the world? We— …."

Lamar rolled over and turned on the lamp.

"One second, Sugar. Hold that thought…."

He reached for his ever-present pad and pen.

After making a few notes, he turned back and tried to excuse his behavior. "Sorry, I had to make a quick note. I was afraid I'd forget. You understand…. What were you saying?"

"Nothing, nothing of any apparent significance, anyway. We'll talk about this another time when you're focused. Get some rest."

Rosemary turned her back to Lamar. She laid in the dark with her eyes open and feigned sleep.

It was the middle of the week before Davey O'Brien finally got a meeting with the busy Bert Bell. Davey was short for a former quarterback, but his broad shoulders, big bones, and long fingers were made for throwing footballs downfield.

"I can't jump leagues, Davey. It's unethical."

"Why is it unethical?"

"A good commissioner must be an impartial guardian of the integrity of both the game and the players. How's it gonna look if I switch leagues? If a fan doubts the integrity of the game or if an owner tampers with the outcome of a game, followers won't find the answer in the sports pages or magazines. It's the commissioner who patrols those sidelines. But Hunt has perfect timing and a great idea. This country's ready for expansion, not a doubt in my mind. It's just not for me."

"Okay, if you can't, you can't. Mr. Hunt thought that a meeting with you would be worth a try. Do me one favor, will you, Bert? Keep all this talk about the new league quiet. A leak could embarrass any potential investors."

"Don't worry, Davey. You have my word. Anything said inside my office stays inside my office."

"I was counting on your integrity, Bert. Thanks."

The two shook hands. As soon as Davey O'Brien left the office, Bell's hand lifted the phone.

CHAPTER NINE

A few feet from a sprawling picture window overlooking Chesapeake Bay was a conference table with a blue leather top and an expensive intercom. The walls were painted a soft dove gray, with color lithograph reproductions of Degas ballet sketches, alongside great moments in Baltimore Colts history, hung around the room.

Rosenbloom sipped a scotch and got down to business. Rooney, Modell, and Mara paid rapt attention.

"I think Bell's too cozy with this other league. They even offered him the commissioner's job. I don't like it. It's time for a change."

"Ah, Carroll, Bell's all right," Modell said. "He handled that betting scandal we had in '46. He saved—"

"He's headstrong. I've known him longer than you," Carroll snapped. "When—"

Art Rooney cut him short. "Bell's judgment has served us well so far. I vote we give him a puncher's chance." Rooney was the oldest in the room, barrel-chested with short, squat legs and thick white brows that met over his nose.

"No one's questioning his judgment, but we pay his salary. We should make the decisions," Carroll said. "We need a more pliable commissioner, someone who'll do as he's told. I think we need to make a change, but go ahead, bring Bell in. Let's hear what he has to say."

Bert Bell, large, confident and bulldog-jowled, marched into the office. "I guess Art's told you boys the news about the new league."

"We heard it, and we don't like it," Carroll said. "More importantly, neither do the boys in Chicago, Cleveland, New York, or

Philly. Do what you have to, but squash this league. These goobers don't know anything about pro football."

Carroll belted his scotch again and said as an afterthought. "Anyone who wants to fuck Carroll Rosenbloom had better be wearing nylons."

Bell smirked and plonked himself into a chair.

"Carroll, simmer down and listen," Bell said. "This league comes at the perfect time. Congress claims that we violate their antitrust laws. You're looking at this wrong. You must look through both sides of the telescope. Hunt's new league will give us cover and further prove that we're not a monopoly."

"Don't we have enough muscle on the Hill to take care of that shit?"

"This Democrat, Emanuel Celler, can't be muscled, a trustbuster, a regular Boy Scout," Bell said. "Believe me, fellows, for now, embrace them. We can always squash them after they've served our purpose."

"Bert, we go back a long time. I respect your opinion and know that you have the league's best interest at heart. I'm going to recommend that you get your way here. Perhaps you're right. You've certainly thrown a new wrinkle into the argument. Thanks for coming down here today. Give us a little time to talk this over and take a vote. Believe me, one thing that we all agree on is that when you go up against Congress, you'll need every advantage possible."

Bell stood, shook Carroll's hand, nodded to the others, turned, and left the office. As soon as the door closed, Carroll pivoted.

"Bert needs to grow a pair of balls. I say we squash this twerp Hunt first and then take our chances with Congress."

"I'm in a 100 percent agreement that we have to keep total control of the league," Modell said. "I certainly don't want to be the one to tell the wise guys in New York that we can't clue them in on at least one game each week, but maybe Bell's right. Congress could be more dangerous to our league than Hunt. Once they start snooping around, who knows where it will end? I think on this issue, Bert's right. Let's deal with Congress first, the new league later."

Art Rooney chimed in with his slight Irish brogue. "Ah, sure, I agree with Modell." His eyes were green and intelligent, his hair white and thinning with a flush to his face because of age and blood pressure. "Hunt folds easy enough. Congress first."

"Art's right," Tim Mara said. "Congress first."

"All right, all right. If that's how you boys feel," Carroll said. "It's your funerals. Tell Bell to make his case before Congress. As soon as that's over, I'm going to steamroll these pissants. We about done here?" He looked around to a series of nods. "Good. I've got a date with a lady."

CHAPTER TEN

It was the end of that week when a disappointed Lamar sat in his Dallas office across from an apologetic Davey O'Brien.

"Thanks, Davey. You tried. I know that we'll have a fight on our hands. I just hope that this doesn't get too malicious. At least Bell said that he'll keep it quiet. That's something."

"He gave me his word."

When the phone rang, Lamar looked at the blinking light, narrowed his left brow, and scowled.

"I told my secretary no calls."

He excused himself and pushed line one.

"What? Sure, of course, Louise. Put her through."

The skin on the corners of his eyes tightened.

"When? This weekend? Rosemary, honey, I can't. I have appointments. Yes. I know it's your mom and dad, but you must understand how important this is. I'll do whatever—"

Rosemary hung up mid-sentence. Lamar cradled the phone, looked across his desk, and lifted his shoulder in a half shrug.

"I'm sorry you had to see that, Davey. My home life unfortunately is in a bit of turmoil. A lot of people think that we rich get away with murder; that money cures all problems. Between my family responsibilities, this new league, and my other interests, sometimes I think I should have a clone. Maybe if there were two of me...."

"No need to apologize. I understand."

"No. You really don't, Davey, and my wife doesn't, either. No one knows what it is to live in the shadow of the richest man in America. No matter what I do, I'll always be H.L. Hunt's son. That's not good enough. I have to be my own man. It sounds crazy for a twenty-seven-year-old man, but I want my own legacy."

The NFL had other ideas.

—⟋⟍⟍⟍—

Unique among American cities, Washington, D.C., was chosen by the Founding Fathers to serve as our nation's capitol. Only a short distance from where the fortunate make the laws, which the unfortunate must abide by, rests George Washington's palatial estate at Mount Vernon. Even back then, the city bearing our first president's name was entangled in political maneuvering, sectional conflicts, issues of race, national identity, compromise, and, of course, the distribution of power and privilege.

A scrutinized Bert Bell sat stiffly at a table in front of a Senate subcommittee hearing headed by liberal New York Congressman Emanuel Celler.

"My concern, Mr. Bell, is that two of the most glamorous industries in the world, television and football, have produced an alliance that will have staggering influence in the future," Celler said. "I'm concerned that pro football will provide the circuses that entertain the hordes while their civic responsibilities dissipate. The more time that our citizens spend in imaginary worlds, the less time they will have to educate themselves about the real one."

"I think you're overestimating our importance, Senator. We're not living in ancient Rome, and if we are a circus, we won't be the only one. H.L. Hunt's son is starting a new football league that will field eight or nine teams, and in the true spirit of American free enterprise, we welcome the competition. I don't have all of their names, but one thing's certain, the names on the list I do have aren't short of money."

Bell handed the list to a committee clerk. After studying the list a few moments, Celler raised an impressed eyebrow and passed it to the other members of the committee.

"That's quite a list, Mr. Bell, but my concern here is the long-term consequences of your league. You want this Congress to hand a small band of persuasive promoters a totally unregulated monopoly. A monopoly, which—in my view—could promote illegal gambling and might even eventually lead to pay television."

"It's the television networks that furnish us our revenue, Senator. Pay TV is a fantasy that will never happen. As for gambling, we diligently police our league with a zero-tolerance policy. As commissioner, the last thing I want is our league to be associated with illegal gambling."

Celler scowled and squinted his right eye.

"It seems to me that football's alliance with television will only encourage betting. Not everyone goes to the stadium to watch a game, but if you bring a game into their living room, well...."

Scrunching his nose while pushing aside a pile of papers he said, "We're going to adjourn for lunch and give our committee time to study this document you submitted." He banged his gavel and stood. "This hearing will reconvene at 2 p.m."

When the Senators reentered chambers, cameras clicked. The crowd fidgeted in their seats. The court officer asked all to rise. Celler drank from a glass of water before asking Bell to stand.

"Despite your diligent argument for this campaign and your league's self-professed purity, I've done my research," he said. "Gambling provides organized crime with their largest source of revenue. I sincerely hope that your league, whether intentionally or unintentionally, doesn't justify my fears and cause the perpetuation of this dangerous vice. I would be inclined to deny this motion, but it seems my colleagues have overruled my objections."

He held up the document that Bell submitted.

"Based on this evidence you've shown us about this competitive new league, I'm going to allow the NFL to continue as an entity and not consider your initiative a monopoly. Go ahead and play your games, Commissioner Bell, but Congress will monitor all future developments of your 'league' very carefully."

CHAPTER ELEVEN

A balmy Florida wind rattled through the dry palm fronds that shielded the sandy shore of Golden Beach. From the restaurant's timber deck, Carroll and Georgia listened to the lapping waves and watched as the orange sun slipped slowly into the horizon before disappearing and mirroring itself across the blue-green capping surface of the water.

Carroll's dark clothes gave the accurate impression he was part Vegas and part Hollywood. He sipped a scotch while she nursed a violent-colored tropical concoction from a tall glass dripping with condensation.

"Very good, sir, your appetizers will be out in a minute."

After the waiter secured the wine list and left the table, Carroll fixated on the large window overlooking the water. Georgia studied Carroll's arresting face, high cheekbones, deep-set eyes, strong jaw, and sharp, flaring nostrils. With a relaxed, polite and smooth manner, his voice lapsed into a confident semi-Southern drawl.

"I hope you didn't mind me ordering for you. I come here all the time." He lifted a glass to his lips and said, "So, tell me something about Sweet Georgia."

She sat demurely with her hands in her lap below a deep cleavage, which showed half her breasts.

"Not that much to tell, Carroll. You're a powerful man. Compared to you, I guess my life is a bit mundane. Most men find me too strong-willed, too ambitious. Maybe that's why I've been married four times."

"I know all about your previous marriages," Carroll said. "What about your current marriage? That's not working out, either?"

"You know all about my previous marriages?" Georgia sneered. "Maybe I shouldn't tell you about myself? Maybe I should let you go ahead and tell me about myself...."

"I apologize for my frankness. I have to be extremely careful about my inner circle." Carroll smiled. "I've worked hard to get where I am today. From what I can tell, you're nobody's fool, either."

Georgia lifted the white cloth napkin from the table, spread it on her lap, and bent her eyes toward it.

"If you're so happy at home, why call me?"

He smiled again.

"My wife and I are separated, heading for a divorce.... When I met you at Joe Kennedy's, I don't know. Something clicked." Carroll paused to sip more scotch, and his eyes narrowed. "Believe me, I tried not to call. The last thing I need is a woman like you."

"A woman like me?"

The waiter delivered the appetizer. "Enjoy your oysters. Your entrée will be out shortly."

Carroll waited until the waiter was out of earshot.

"I mean a woman as irresistible as you: bright, beautiful, seductive. You're like an opiate. One taste of Georgia could be addictive."

"The answer seems simple enough." Her eyes sparkled. "Don't bite from the forbidden fruit."

"Look you're too smart to play games with. I know your history." Carroll paused to dab horseradish on an oyster. He squeezed lemon onto the oyster and then carefully let it slide into his open mouth. "I don't know where this thing will end up, but I'll risk it if you will."

"I'm not here to play games, either. Powerful men excite me. I want to see as much of you as I can."

Georgia slowly, seductively consumed an oyster.

"Of course, I understand there will be no strings, but outside of my husband, I won't see anybody else. You don't mind, do you?"

"If your husband can live with that, you won't get any complaints from me."

The restaurant's piano player began to play "As Time Goes By." After a long, instrumental introduction, he crooned, "You must remember this...."

As Georgia listened, her mind drifted with the music. Her gaze looked through a hole in the dimension at a twenty-seven-year-old memory in St. Louis.

—∿—

Surrounding a car lot in the middle of the Oklahoma Dust Bowl, signs and balloons signified a grand opening crammed with brand-new 1932 model cars. On a makeshift stage, a fourteen-piece, all-women's band played outside the car lot's entrance. The A-frame read, "Lucia Pamela and her Musical Pirates."

The stunning blonde conducting the orchestra positively glowed while basking in the crowd's attention. Watching the festivities, a five-year-old Georgia stared wide-eyed and used a small stick to mimic her mother's baton, her beat-up teddy bear cast aside in the Okie mud.

Not far from those pleasant memories were other recollections, the image of a sniffling, frightened child, hugging that same teddy bear while her drunken parents argued in the front room of their downtrodden trailer.

"Broken-down towns and broken-down venues, that's where hooking up with a loser like you got me," Lucia said. "I could be playing New York or Chicago instead of traveling around in this tin can. I was so stupid to get pregnant. If it weren't for you and Georgia, I'd be living the high life."

"Thank your stars for that little girl," Georgia's daddy said. "You're not fit to be her mother. If not for her, I would have left you years ago. You should act more like her mother and less like her employer. She'd be a great deal happier."

"You're a deadbeat and a loser. You're no father to her nor husband to me. You disgust me."

Then something in Georgia's mind clicked like a camera. She saw her father's large, square hand go up in the air. She saw it come down hard against her mother's face. She could still hear the sounds of her weeping....

Georgia let the sour taste of her childhood memories linger a few moments longer before shifting her focus back to the restaurant, Carroll, and 1959.

Carroll was jabbering something about how he had made his money on a dungaree contract with the government during the war and how wealth was easier wheedled out of groups as opposed to individuals.

"The government steals from the common man. Once they've accumulated the people's money, I finagle it from them. It's simple, really."

Georgia had drifted and missed the gist of his conversation. Rather than appearing bored, it was simpler to switch the subject.

"Sorry, you don't mind if I smoke, do you?"

"No, not at all," Carroll said. "I smoke occasionally, but a beautiful woman like you doesn't need a cigarette between those lovely lips."

"Oh? And what does a beautiful woman like me need between my lovely lips?"

Carroll deliberated a short moment, devoured Georgia with his eyes, smiled, and surrendered to impulse.

"Suddenly, I'm not that hungry. What do you say I get the check, and we get the hell out of here?"

CHAPTER TWELVE

Lamar hollered through the phone.

"No way Bell pulled that stunt in front of Congress on his own, Bud. He was well coached by his masters."

"We'll have to ditch the whole shooting match," Adams said. "To go ahead now would be suicidal. By announcing our plans, they're forcing us to accelerate our schedule. We're not ready. We'd be like blind pigs. All we did was help them beat their antitrust suit. They played us for suckers."

"You go ahead and quit if you want," Lamar said. "They're not getting rid of me that easy. I'm more determined now than ever. I'm so ticked off that I can barely see."

Lamar lifted the newspaper off his desk and had a moment of clarity.

"Hang on a second, Bud. Maybe, just maybe, they overplayed their hand. I'm looking at today's Times. The front page reads, 'Bell tells Congress about new football league.' If I had announced our new league, it never would have received this much coverage. It certainly wouldn't be plastered across the front page."

"It's your call," Adams said. "This whole thing was your idea, but if you carry on, you'll have to get tough with these bastards. With them, business ain't just business. It's a contact sport."

Lamar's face stiffened.

"You're right, of course. I was naïve to think they'd play by any set of rules. They've underestimated me too, dang it. From this day on, I'll swap my Bible for *The Art of War*. Those are the rules that I'll play by now. Trust me. We'll carry on, and some day they'll regret that they took Lamar Hunt so lightly. I'll make this work … no matter what it takes, so help me God."

———**w**———

In a Dallas delivery room where Rosemary had given birth to Lamar's second child, the screams and tears were long gone. Rosemary poked her index finger though the pink blanket in which her baby was swaddled. She held Lamar's daughter against her breast with a determined glint in her eye and a brave smile on her face.

Littering her private room, boxes of candy were lost in what looked like a rainforest of flowers. But like a funeral parlor, the orchids only served to make the room sadder and Rosemary's eyes colder.

Lamar finally met his daughter when she was three hours old.

———**w**———

Days later, with the baby safely snuggling in her crib, Rosemary poured her heart out to Lamar. She sat up in their bed, turned on the light, and said, "You have to curb this obsession of a new league, Lamar. I hardly know you anymore. Years ago, we were up on a mountain. We were up so high, Lamar. We had it all. I never dreamed that I could ever feel like that. When we got married, we sealed it forever, indelible, forever no matter what happened. We had more than any two people in the world deserve. You changed all that. I feel like the kids and I are no longer your main priority."

"Of course, you're my main priority. Without my family, it will all be for nothing. From now on, I promise. My family will always come first. Turn out your lamp and get some sleep. We'll work this out, sugar."

Within six months, Rosemary and Lamar would be separated and headed for a divorced.

CHAPTER THIRTEEN

L amar and Bud Adams stood behind a lectern at the latest summit of the presumptive ownership group. Standing next to them was Joe Foss, the most celebrated Marine ace of World War II.

"Bud, why don't ya go ahead and introduce our prospective commissioner to the boys."

"Gentlemen, Joe Foss here can help us a lot," Adams said. "He's a Congressional Medal of Honor winner, one of the top two deadliest Marines to ever sit in the cockpit of a fighter plane and blast the living shit out of the enemies of freedom, democracy, and everything that's decent. Why, he's the only man who ever survived a head-on collision with a Japanese Zero. We'll be goddamn lucky to get him. I'll go ahead and let him tell y'all about himself, then y'all can decide for yourselves."

The smiling Foss sauntered to the lectern inadvertently fumigating the conference room with an object between his teeth that resembled a cigar. He removed the soppy dinge from his mouth.

"I don't know who Mr. Adams is talking about. He's got my name right, but far as I know, no fighter pilot has ever survived a head-on collision with a Japanese Zero or any other type of aircraft for that matter."

Foss grinned like a game show host while all the sitting men smiled politely. He wore tan slacks with a brown tweed jacket and a red striped tie.

"First off, let me be up front. I'm no football genius. You fellas don't need one." He waved the cigar stub in his right hand like a baton. "Your organization needs to sell a product. I can do that. You give me five minutes, and I can sell the pope a double bed."

That garnered genuine laughs.

"My mantra is simple. When you get into something, get into it all the way. I was born in a crappy little farmhouse in Sioux Falls, South Dakota. Electricity was so new to us that when I was seventeen, my daddy went out and got himself killed by it, so I had to take over the family farm. When I wasn't plowing fields, taking care of my siblings, or working at the local gas station, I managed to get my pilot's license and log over 100 hours of flight time." Foss exhibited a hero's swagger, which only highlighted his plain talk and rugged good looks. Those three traits combined with his winning smile exuded confidence and enthusiasm.

"Once my brother was old enough to run the farm, I enrolled in the University of South Dakota, where I boxed, ran track, played football, bussed tables, and logged as much flight time as I could. Before joining the Marines, I got my degree in business administration and served as a private in the National Guard. I'm not sophisticated, but I'm certainly no stranger to hard work. I'll bust my country ass twenty-four hours a day, seven days a week, and crisscross the borders of this great country to sell your new league."

He placed the cigar stub between his teeth and spread both palms.

"That's about the long and the short of it, but no matter how you gentlemen decide, remember I'm not kidding. I'm a born salesman. My momma used to tell her friends that her little boy Joe could sell ketchup lollipops to women in white dresses."

Hunt basked under the glow of Foss's integrity.

"Joe, I can't speak for everyone in this room, but you've certainly sold me. As far as I'm concerned, our league doesn't need a legislator. We need to sell our product, and you're absolutely perfect."

The AFL had found its new commissioner.

—⚉—

Their new commissioner selected, one day after Hunt's twenty-seventh birthday, an apprehensive duo assembled three dozen or so media members in Adam's Houston "office." Adam's subterranean retreat was complete with a barbecue pit, lily pond, and a desk as long as a bowling alley.

Flanked by Adams, Lamar took the podium.

"I would like to announce that beginning in the fall of 1960, the American Football League will begin playing in eight cities nationwide and directly compete with the NFL. Our fan-friendly new league will play fourteen games and be built for excitement. This will be a passing league not one dominated by a running game."

One gruff reporter shouted, "What cities? Why now? And why go head-to-head with the NFL?"

"Dallas and Houston will be first," Lamar said. "Bud will run the Houston franchise, and I will run Dallas's. As for your second and third questions, America's appetite for football has outgrown what the NFL can deliver. We tried bargaining, and they denied us, so we are starting our own league."

"Where will you get the players?" another shouted.

"There are plenty of great players out there," Lamar said. "And I don't just mean white players. Negro colleges have fine players. If they're competitive, the AFL wants them."

"What about coaches?"

"Lots of fine coaches don't have jobs." Lamar laughed. "We are going to create a lot of jobs in football."

"Who will the other owners be?"

"We are not at liberty to say at this time, but they are all heavy hitters whose names you'll recognize" Lamar said. "I can assure you. We are just dotting i's and crossing t's here. We will get you those names in the coming weeks. You guys will have total access to everything we do. No secrets." Lamar bent his head in Adams's direction. "Bud, would you like to add anything?"

Adams ambled to the mic and surveyed the crowd. Knowing that the fastest way to a reporter's heart was a free lunch, he eyeballed the lavish buffet aside the open bar and said, "Lamar and I will stick around to answer any questions, fellas. I don't know about you, but I'm hungry. The AFL is buying. Let's eat."

CHAPTER FOURTEEN

An impeccably dressed Carroll and the characteristically drab Lamar watched the Baltimore Colts game on a Sunday afternoon from Rosenbloom's private box. Near the end of the first quarter, the scoreboard read Baltimore 7, Pittsburgh 0.

"Thanks for inviting me, Carroll. When your Colts played in Dallas, I became a huge fan," Lamar said. "They are still my favorite NFL team. Did I tell you that Raymond Berry played ahead of me at SMU?"

"No, you didn't. No wonder you couldn't crack their first string." Rosenbloom flashed a broad smile before the sound of his phone distracted him. "Excuse me a second."

Rosenbloom lifted the phone but said nothing. With Carroll busy, Lamar opened his wallet and shifted his attention to a picture of Rosemary and the kids. A tear momentarily streaked his cheeks. He repocketed his wallet and caught the end of Carroll's conversation.

"Thanks, Gerry. Remember, I want those scores every five minutes. All right, remember, every five minutes."

Rosenbloom cradled the phone and turned to Lamar.

"I like to keep abreast of what's going on around the league. You were saying you played behind Berry at SMU? I played a little football myself, but swimming is my game."

Carroll lit a cigarette.

"I've never seen you smoke before," Lamar said.

"Only on game days. I get a little nervous," Carroll said.

Carroll dragged on his cigarette and scrutinized Lamar. "Look, let's stop the bullshit. Give up this nonsense about a new league, and I'll get you that Dallas franchise you were after."

"Now? … Now you want to give me a franchise. What about the cost of airfares between Dallas and the Northeast? How will the other owners feel about that?"

"The other owners will do whatever I say; besides, that new television contract has made us financially solvent. Airline fares will be the least of our worries."

"What about my other partners and their teams? I gave them my word. That means something to me." Lamar cleared his throat. "You'll have to accept all the teams in our league or no deal."

"All your teams? You have no fuckin' teams," Carroll said. "You only have concepts. And you gave them your word? Fuck your word. This is business."

Rosenbloom took a swig of his drink before trying another tact.

"Look, Lamar, I'm not inflexible. I believe I speak for the other owners. How about we absorb four teams: Dallas, Houston, Buffalo, and Minnesota? That's my last offer and a damn good one. You'd be smart to take it."

"No. You listen, Carroll. I list my home phone number publicly. I don't hide from anyone. I pride myself on that. That comes from not just having a conscience but making decisions based on it. I'll never break my word to my partners."

"Fuck your conscience, and fuck your ethics. You want success? Fuck them before they fuck you."

Lamar had heard enough. Before he headed for the exit, he mustered a retort.

"Thanks for the advice. Now I'll give you some of my dad's. Character decides your fate, not money, not ambition…. At this moment, I wouldn't gamble a whole lot on yours."

As Lamar headed to the exit, Carroll was about to scream a comeback but then the phone rang again. He ignored Lamar to focus on the updated scores.

—m—

In his enormous office, Bud Adams drawled into the phone. "Rosenbloom, that surely is a generous offer. Damn straight,

$650,000 is a bargain for a Houston franchise, but I gave my word to Hunt." He listened into the earpiece and answered, "Yes, my word means something. No, not just something. In Texas, it means everything."

"Don't give me that," Carroll said. "I don't want to listen to any more of that 'a man is only as good as his word' bullshit."

"It's a pity that you don't understand the concept ... all the more reason we can't do business, Mr. Rosenbloom."

Rosenbloom lost his patience and screamed into the phone.

"You realize what I'm offering you? The NFL has been down this road before. You can't compete with us. You'll be out of business by the end of the year."

"I've made bad decisions before. Mistakes don't scare me. When all is said and done, at the very least, bad decisions make for great yarns around a bottle of bourbon. Have a nice day, Rosenbloom, and thanks again for the offer."

Never one to be intimidated, Bud Adams slammed the phone down in Carroll's ear.

CHAPTER FIFTEEN

In the middle of the conference table, the newspaper headline read, "Oct 11, 1959—NFL Commissioner Bert Bell Dies."

"No one in this room will miss Bert more than me," Rosenbloom said. "At least Bell died doing what he loved. Shit, he was watching an Eagles–Steelers game. That's all any of us can ask. I pray that he rests in peace.... That said, life goes on. We don't need to replace Bell as commissioner. We don't need anybody to tell us how to run our own game. We need a PR man with the title of commissioner. Right now, we need to grow unrestricted and, I mean, unrestricted. We need someone who'll protect our interests, not compromise them like Bert did by allowing this new league to hatch. I've asked the Rams general manager, Pete Rozelle, to come down today. He's perfect—smooth, articulate, and super savvy about marketing. If we hire him, he promises television growth and a move toward full attendance. Most importantly, he'll crush Hunt's league."

Rosenbloom spoke into his intercom.

"Vera, send Mr. Rozelle in, please."

A tall, slim- statured, impeccably dressed man entered. His forehead was high. His skin fine grained, his smile easy and good-natured. After preliminary amenities, his rather prominent nose found itself behind the lectern.

"Broadcasting has ushered in a new era," Rozelle said. "Televisions will someday flood every home in America. Football must grow along with the medium. When we sign future contracts with the networks, we must demand total marketing control, even to what commentators we allow to announce our games.... Also, we can't allow competition. This other league must go."

The intercom interrupted Rozelle.

"Mr. Rosenbloom, you have a call on line three."

"Vera, I told you to hold all calls."

"I told the caller you were in a conference. She said it was urgent."

"Excuse me, boys. I better take this."

Striding to a corner desk, he pushed the button labeled three.

"Carroll Rosenbloom."

"Baby, I had to call you."

"Yes?" he whispered.

"I was sitting here thinking about last night. I'm dripping wet and needed to hear a powerful man's voice."

"Well, I'm in a meeting right now...."

"I won't keep you. Just listen a moment. I'm sitting here with my fingers inside my panties. Oh, yes, baby, baby, listen, yes, baby. Oh my God, you drive me crazy."

Flushed, Carroll managed a slight smile. "Well, thank you for that information. I'll clear my schedule."

"Clear your schedule? I'm clearing every surface in the house. I can't wait to see you tonight.... Go ahead, honey. Limp back to your meeting." Wearing cutoff dungaree shorts and a pink sweatshirt, Georgia chuckled, cradled the phone, and turned a page of Cosmopolitan.

Carroll talked into the dead phone.

"Yes. Goodbye now, and thanks for that information. We'll discuss it tomorrow."

Carroll returned to the conference table in time to hear the end of Rozelle's presentation. Rozelle's thin, brown hair was styled over a high forehead. It grew slightly over his collar, giving him a craggy, casual look.

"I was the sports director at CBS before I worked for the Rams. One thing I can promise you, I can make sure that my friends there don't announce any AFL scores. That'll help undermine their credibility."

Carroll interrupted him.

"I'm sure you boys have a lot of questions for Pete. I'm not rushing the process, but the sooner we elect a new commissioner, the sooner we can announce our plans for expansion."

"Expansion? What expansion?" Modell asked.

"I said grow—unimpeded," Rosenbloom answered.

In his new capacity as commissioner, Pete Rozelle confirmed Rosenbloom's plans to a group of reporters.

"Next year the NFL will expand into the following nine cities: Dallas, Houston, Minneapolis, Boston, Buffalo, Miami, Louisville, Denver, and New Orleans."

Rozelle was a buoyant, chain-smoking, cocktail-sipping PR man who exuded class and confidence. He would go on to become one of the most transformational commissioners in the history of sports. His mix of personal charm, toughness, business foresight, and political savvy would steer the league through a remarkable period of growth and prosperity. It would help transition the league through the global turmoil of the '60s and '70s.

A reporter checked his notes and yelled out a question.

"Commissioner, aren't those all potential AFL cities?"

"The antitrust laws provide that all states are fair territory. Let's face it. They're moving into L.A. and New York. We have teams there. We're not complaining. Competition provides Americans choices. The NFL has always been about free enterprise and choice. After all, we're not communists."

"But why expansion now, commissioner?"

"Why not expansion now? That's all for now, boys. I've got another meeting."

At an emergency meeting, Hunt and the members of the new league sat around a conference table, stunned at Pete Rozelle's announcement.

"They're not fooling anybody. By expanding into every AFL city, they've declared war on our league in front of 200 million people."

Lamar picked up his yellow pad and made a quick notation.

"We might have gotten a fair shake with Bell. Rosenbloom hired this guy Rozelle to crush us."

The noise outside the conference room turned everybody's head. Harry Wismer burst through the door, carrying several newspapers. Harry ranted and raved a few seconds before glaring directly at Max Winter's conspicuously empty seat.

"We have a Judas in our midst, boys, and he's raised his ugly head. This looks like it could be our Last Supper."

Wismer hurled the stack of newspapers into the center of the table. The headline read "Minneapolis Gets NFL Franchise."

When Wismer focused on the newspapers, his eyes spat venom. "Max Winter has sold us out."

Lamar lifted the top newspaper off the stack, scanned the headline, and said, "That treacherous son of a bitch just wrecked our schedule. Without Minnesota, we'll only have seven teams and an unbalanced league. We're being hit from all angles."

"Can we survive this?" Hilton asked.

Lamar hardened his eyes and stared at Hilton.

"We have to survive it. If they think that this will make me quit, they don't know me."

Despite the bravado, Lamar's pulse beat in his throat with the urgency of a damaged watch that was quickly running out of time.

As soon as the other team owners left the conference room, Lamar lifted the phone.

"I ain't bellyaching, Dad. That day when we drove my old Buick through Texas, you warned me that I'd be dealing with some unsavory characters. I just never expected one of my own partners to betray me. Max Winter is taking his Minnesota franchise to the NFL."

"Son, don't be so shocked." H.L. laughed. "Once money is involved, scruples and honor tend to saddle their fastest horses. I've heard too many phonies talk about their honor time and time again. I tell them your honor is all well and good. Now, show me your cash."

"Yeah, but I took these men at their word."

"I always take a man's word and then do a thorough background check," H.L. said. "I don't allow anyone into my inner circle unless I know everything about him. Don't listen to what they say. Watch what they do."

"Well, I've just seen what Winter is made of," Lamar said.

"Don't ever forget what us Hunts are made of either," H.L. said. "I know you want to do this on your own, but I took the liberty of having my people run background checks on these NFL boys. They have shaky pasts, especially Rosenbloom."

"All powerful men have skeletons in their closets," Lamar said.

"Maybe, but Rosenbloom has enough skeletons to open a medical college. In the '50s, Carroll Rosenbloom and some beauty named Lou Chesler loaned their buddy Mike McLaney the money to purchase a large Cuban hotel-casino from, of all people, Meyer Lansky. This fella McLaney is a talented golf and tennis player who refused to turn pro because Rosenbloom is his personal pigeon. He sometimes fleeced that chump out of $250,000 on a single round of golf."

"I already knew Rosenbloom was a heavy gambler. He calls it his hobby," Lamar said.

"The three largest companies Chesler controlled were … wait a second, I've got it right here."

H.L. reached into the breast pocket of his blue serge suit, snatched a piece of loose-leaf paper, and read from it.

"Universal Controls, General Development, and Seven Arts Ltd., the Hollywood production company."

He folded the paper carefully.

"By no coincidence, Chesler's bookie, some guinea hood named "Trigger" Mike Coppola, also owned a large block of General Development stock. This guy Chesler often bet as much as $500,000 on a horse race with Coppola. Your boy Rosenbloom was not only the second-largest stockholder in Seven Arts but was also a corporate officer in all three of Chesler's companies."

"I've heard the rumors."

"I don't deal in rumors, son. These are facts. When the gambling casinos were shut down after Fidel Castro's revolution,

Mike McLaney lost all of Rosenbloom's and Chesler's cash. Castro even threw McLaney in a Havana jail for a while. He's not the only NFL owner with a shaky past. George Halas's Chicago Bears were bankrolled by a known crony of Al Capone. Rooney is a prominent Pittsburgh gambler. Art Modell has reported ties to the Cleveland Mob. The list goes on and on."

H.L. took the sheet of paper and placed it back in his pocket to save for his son.

"Thanks, Dad, I guess I should have done a bit more homework before I started this venture," Lamar said.

"I didn't get to be the richest man in the world by not doing my due diligence." H.L. said.

Lamar was shaken but undaunted.

He knew he was right and had given these men his word. He couldn't concern himself with the character defects of his adversaries. As that traitor Winter had proven, if money started rolling in, it would be tough enough keeping his own laundry clean.

CHAPTER SIXTEEN

In his Baltimore office, Carroll's secretary offered cream and sugar to Clint Murchison. The owner of the newest NFL franchise, the Dallas Cowboys, cradled his mug with both palms while Carroll swallowed his coffee from a tall blue beaker.

"Clint, listen to me. Take my advice. It's imperative that you push up your team's opening date a year. Why let Hunt's team get a foothold in Dallas?"

"The strategy's sound, but we haven't even been approved as a franchise yet."

"That's only a formality. Look, if Hunt's team fails in Dallas, their whole league folds. Their new league kicks off in the fall. It's important that your Dallas franchise starts a year earlier and establishes a foothold in the market. Can you make that happen?"

"Yeah, as long as you can get us approved. I can almost guarantee it. I just hired Tex Schramm away from the Rams. He knows this business inside out. I'm almost positive that we can pull that off."

"Good, then it's settled. I'll tell the other owners you'll be ready to start one year early." Rosenbloom rubbed his hand casually in a slow circular motion across his flat stomach before squinting one of his piercing blue eyes directly at Murchison.

"You might also consider offering SMU's quarterback, Don Meredith, a contract."

"Tex already thought of that, but the rules state we're not permitted to approach college players until after they've played their last game."

"Screw the rules. Go ahead and make him an offer, anyway," Carroll said. "We owners make the rules. You'll find out when you're a part of the club that we do what we need to do to protect ourselves. Let me tell you a quick anecdote. We have a rule in place that the player's union is trying to overturn. It states that veteran players must negotiate their own contracts. The Packers' Jim Ringo tried to ignore it and sent a lawyer to negotiate his contract with Vince Lombardi. Lombardi asked the lawyer to wait while he went into another room. When he returned a few minutes later, he told the lawyer, 'You're negotiating with the wrong club. Mr. Ringo is now with Philadelphia.'

"There's only one rule that's inflexible. No owner can offer a contract to a player already signed with another club. We can't abide that. If we let personal vanity lead to bidding wars, it'll interfere with sound fiscal policy, and we'll all go broke. Our owners have huge egos and cut each other's throats all the time. Many of us don't even like each other, but if something like that were to happen, you'd see an alliance that would almost be touching. We don't hijack other team's players. Other than that, there's not much I can't push through."

That same day, Lamar and his new commissioner, Joe Foss, met at a roadside barbeque joint where the food was good and the jukebox even better. In her emotive yet distant voice, Patsy Cline was falling to pieces while Lamar, choosing to ignore her, squirted ketchup and mustard on a burger that might have passed as a loin of brontosaurus.

He put the last stroke on the masterpiece by placing the heel of his hand on the top of the bun and pressing down hard. Before lifting it, he said, "This is the way we've got to run our drafts, Joe. If a top prospect comes out of a college in that team's geographical area, then that team will have first rights to draft him. A territorial draft ensures that local stars play in the arenas where they became famous. That will place enough fannies in the seats to benefit the collective good."

"That's sound thinking, Lamar," Foss said. "That'll sell tickets for sure. Football players are gods in the South."

"After SMU plays its last game, I'll offer Don Meredith a contract. He's a personal friend. That sucker alone will sell out the Cotton Bowl. It won't matter who we're playing."

Ever careless about his diet, Lamar chugged a large root beer while he swallowed a bite of his burger.

"In two weeks, Harry Wismer and I will meet with ABC about a possible contract. We need this deal desperately and not just because of the money. Television will give us the exposure...."

"How good are Harry's television connections?"

"They better be damn good. Without this contract, we're as dead as Jefferson Davis. When they announced expansion, I should have sent my lawyer after those unethical bastards. I'd have owned their league. Wherever we tried to start a team, they started a team. Talk about antitrust—before our proposal those gangsters didn't have a team south of D.C. Dad was right. I better keep my guard up around these fellas. The higher they reach, the lower they'll go. They'll take the eyes out of our heads and say we look better without them."

CHAPTER SEVENTEEN

A week later, the light flipped green, and Lamar slowly eased his rented Buick behind the bumper of the taxicab in front of him. In Manhattan, where stop signs and traffic lights are mere suggestions, he turned left on Seventh Avenue to beat the traffic and ended up hitting more. This meeting with ABC executives in New York was one he didn't want to be late for. To ease the tension, he spun the radio to a sports station and was rewarded with more stress.

"And in the last of the NBA scores, Boston led by Bill Russell's 17 points and 23 rebounds beat the Knicks 125–110. Moving along now to football news, the Dallas Cowboys announced the signing today of quarterback Don Meredith. According to Cowboy General Manager Tex Schramm, the former SMU star will be the cornerstone of the newest NFL franchise."

Lamar stiffened. His heart missed a beat and then it began pounding so hard that he had to breathe deeply to quiet it. His eyes became fierce slits, and behind those slits, you could almost see him drawing a rake through his thoughts. It was clear to Lamar that truth and trust came with his faith, but this other league didn't worship at the same altar. He could either obey the rules and lose everything, or he could change.

He gritted his teeth and tried to let all the fatigue, heat, and anger drain from his hands and feet. He was genuinely and uncharacteristically wired, wrapped so tight that his skin felt like a prison. He pulled into the first open parking spot and turned off the radio. His face quivered as though he had been shocked, then the thousands of tiny wrinkles in his face flattened with rage. He began pounding the dashboard with his fists.

—⟋⟍—

Before entering Wismer's New York apartment, Lamar parked his car in a Midtown garage and rehashed his thoughts about what was at stake. All previous competition to the NFL had failed to survive because of lack of revenue. Television dollars could change that and be his league's salvation. Lamar was well aware that if this morning's meeting with the two representatives from cash-starved ABC didn't go well that the league's fortunes would change for the worse.

His host for the meeting, Harry Wismer, was erratic and unpredictable. Harry loved confusing people. He'd meet someone, immediately say congratulations, and then walk away, leaving the person mystified as to what they had done to be congratulated.

"Everyone has done something they're proud of," he reasoned.

He once entered a crowded room and just to gauge reactions said, "So, they finally shot Castro?" Harry just loved to keep people off balance.

—⟋⟍—

Sitting at Wismer's kitchen table, Harry and Lamar represented the new league. Edgar Scherick and Thomas Moore represented ABC. To avoid media scrutiny, that threesome arrived inside Harry Wismer's apartment at three different times.

"We are prepared to offer your network our total AFL package for $2 million a year," Wismer said.

This statement drove ABC's Moore into a fit of mockery.

"Two million a year?"

Moore looked at Scherick and started laughing. Moore was casually dressed in blue sweater and gray slacks. His face was round and bearded. Leaning back on the sofa, he placed his hands behind his head and said calmly, "You're out of your mind, Wismer. I have a job to keep. I was told to offer $200,000 at most."

"What—$200,000? That's ridiculous. It's unacceptable, and frankly insulting. You can take that offer and stick it where the sun don't shine. As a matter of fact, if you and Moore don't leave the room immediately, I will."

The two ABC executives disregarded Harry's ultimatum and began talking to one another. Refusing to be ignored, Wismer screamed, banged the table with his fist, stood in a fury, turned over his chair, and stormed out. In his confusion, instead of charging out the door, he darted into his own closet.

Lamar leaned forward, smiled, and spoke in a low, civil voice to defuse the tension.

"Please excuse Harry. He's a bit theatrical."

The two executives calmed down a bit, and Moore lit a cigarette. By the time Moore extinguished it, Wismer emerged from the closet and sat down as if nothing had happened. He tried a new tact.

"Take into consideration who your sponsors will be," Wismer said. "Football sells cars, beer, and cigarettes. Our product doesn't exactly appeal to little old ladies."

Scherick deliberated Harry's wisdom and huddled with Moore. Within the hour, Scherick and Moore left Wismer's apartment, and the four had an agreement.

"Considering that the other networks wouldn't even negotiate with us, ABC gave us a pretty good deal here," Hunt said. "Notwithstanding the protection clauses, $8.5 million over five years is pretty damn good."

Without hesitating, Wismer then came up with the single most important suggestion to protect the new league.

"As broke as I am, we can't worry about individual profits, Lamar. We should spread this television money equally. That'll help the smaller markets survive. Right now, we must strengthen the league. We're only as strong as our weakest team."

Wismer's foresight of introducing organized socialism proved the smartest thing the fledgling league could have done to ensure parity.

"Considering the financial shape of your New York franchise, that's noble, Harry," Lamar said. "You're absolutely right. We can't be shortsighted. This contract will subsidize each team about $100,000 per year. I'll never be able to thank you enough for your unselfishness and your loyalty to the league, Harry. I'll never forget it."

—∞—

Later that afternoon in a small Midwestern town, the local press assembled in front of a quaint town hall. In a rumpled corduroy suit, a gruff Joe Foss delivered a speech that was part Sioux Falls simplicity and part Madison Avenue public relations. In a show of solidarity, a few members of The Foolish Club were in attendance.

Foss paused to unwrap a cigar.

"After backstabbing negotiations, Minnesota pulled out of our league to join the NFL, so whatever team we allow into the league will inherit their draft picks. Their deliberate treachery in hijacking Minnesota left us with only seven teams. The addition of an extra franchise will rebalance our league. The NFL owners are doing everything in their power to undermine our endeavors. In response, our league is suing the NFL for trying to eliminate competition."

He shoved the unlit cigar in his mouth.

"Their actions are un-American. I didn't fight in WWII to watch this happen. Lamar Hunt and these other AFL owners are underdogs just struggling to survive against this huge monopoly."

One reporter turned to another, "Is this guy on the level, H.L. Hunt's kid is an underdog?"

CHAPTER EIGHTEEN

It was before sunrise that Thursday when two members of The Foolish Club pulled into the golf course. The Dallas sun came up yellow and hot. The mist had barely settled over the first tee, where Barron Hilton stood and chatted with Lamar.

"Now that Max Winter has withdrawn and Minnesota no longer has a franchise, Oakland should be allowed that extra team we need to balance the league. I know other cities want teams, Lamar, but I feel strongly about this. New York and L.A. are our biggest markets. My Chargers need a rivalry to survive. If you don't award California that extra team, I'd have to consider withdrawing from the league."

"Barron, are you threatening me?" Lamar smirked and approached his ball. His soft swing drew the ball 260 yards down the middle of the fairway. He admired his drive, picked up his tee, and smiled.

"I don't cotton to threats, Barron. Blackmailing would never work on me. But just as a point of information, I couldn't agree with you more. Forgive me for not telling you sooner, but I wanted to wait until the deal was finalized. It looks like our league will be welcoming Charlie Soda and F. Wayne Valley as the newest franchise owners in our California market. They signed a tentative agreement, giving them controlling interest in a limited partnership that will purchase a new team in the Bay Area."

Hilton's mind galloped with possibilities. His eyes swept past the main building's parking lot, dwelling a moment to survey the rolling hills, the fairways, and oak trees before focusing back on the task at hand. Hilton stuck a tee in the ground, stood behind his ball to line up his shot, and broke into a wide smile.

"So, you realize that the coasts must have the strongest markets?"

Hilton hit a smooth drive down the fairway. His ball stopped just outside the left rough about 150 yards from the green.

"Nice drive," Lamar said.

As both strolled from the tee toward their cart, Lamar turned to Barron, "I think that it's absolutely crucial that the coastal cities have strong teams. Even more essential is that our overall product must be better than the NFL's. We can't just be as good as them. We've got to be better."

The two men slid into their cart and drove toward their shots.

"If we make enough small changes like the two-point conversion, I think we can change the entire game. The average quarterback in the NFL throws the ball about sixteen times. They've built their reputation on three yards and a cloud of dust. Imagine if quarterbacks threw the ball twice as much. Downfield passes are exciting, damn it. I'm going to do my best to make our league wide open."

Later that evening, Lamar and his father watched on television as Pete Rozelle, the slickest of public relations men, conducted yet another press conference.

"Gentlemen, because our officials only earn $250 a game, some muckrakers suggest that makes them susceptible to bribes. Nothing could be further from the truth. These men do this as a hobby, not for money. The referees and officials of the NFL are bankers, lawyers, and judges, professional men with reputations beyond reproach. They have our league's full confidence."

"Lawyers, judges and bankers are beyond reproach?" H.L. laughed. "That story he just told the press didn't do nothin' but leave skid marks on the bowl. Watch yourself when you deal with that man, son. He's either a fool or a liar. The more he rants about the official's integrity and howls against legalized gambling, the more I think I was a sucker for ever laying a dime on a football game. If his league is against gambling, why do they release injury reports, field conditions, and point spreads every week? If people can't bet legitimately, how will they bet? The same way I do, over the phone with bookies. Think about it. If you were a crook, wouldn't you hire a slick, glib public relations man, who appears squeaky clean, to represent you? Well, wouldn't you?"

"Don't get yourself all worked up, Dad," Lamar said. "No sense changing the habits of a lifetime now. You've always put a few dollars on a game or two, and you always will."

"Son, let me tell you something. I'm no Aristotle, but after seventy-five years on the planet, I've found that where money's involved, nothing's on the level: not churches, not governments, not wars, nothing. If the little guy wants a seat at the table, he better cough up some serious cash. Let me tell you something else. The more money on the table, the less chance the little guy has of ever sitting at it."

"Where's all this going, Dad? Have you suddenly become a crusader, or is there a point to all of this?"

"You have to be damn careful of this crowd you're gonna be in bed with. Men with sketchy pasts are behind some of these teams, and a lot of money is being made illegally. Some of these boys have contacts with organized crime and known gamblers. Shoot, some of them were bookies, racetrack owners, high-rolling sports betters, and even slot machine manufacturers. The public perceives professional sports as absolutely on the level. Fans think money doesn't influence the game. That gambling is only a side effect."

"Gambling is a side effect of the sport," Lamar said.

"No, gambling is the sport. It's even more American than football. It's what drives football. I've been betting Saturdays all my life. If this new league of yours is to succeed, it will be because of gambling, not in spite of it. You've got to ensure that your referees have impeccable integrity. That will be tough."

Lamar focused on his father's sermon.

"Millions crave their fix every Sunday. Big-time mobbed-up gamblers have made inroads and influenced the game. The opportunity for fixes and huge betting coups are glossed over. You will have to ensure that your product is as clean as cotton."

Lamar took out his pad and made a note.

"You know, Dad, it's funny you should bring that up. Just last week, I was talking to Harry Wismer. He said pretty much the same thing. Wismer said that in the two decades since he's been broadcasting, some strange stuff has left him uneasy: a questionable penalty, an interception in the flat, a quarterback eating the ball for a sack when he could have thrown the ball away. He swore up and down that it's nearly impossible for a football play to be run without an infraction of some kind. Holding is the usual call, and officials could probably call it every time a play is run. It's certainly disconcerting. Maybe we should make our officials take lie detector tests before games?"

CHAPTER NINETEEN

T he AFL debuted September 9, 1960, with the Denver Broncos edging the Boston Patriots in front of 21,595 people at Nickerson Field. The 13–10 final was hardly the fireworks Lamar had promised.

Still, Hunt's glass was half full as he placed a call to Adams that Saturday morning.

"Encouraging start last night, don't you think, Bud?"

"We didn't put our best foot forward scheduling those two teams for the opener," Adams said. "We'll have to get our studs on the field and score more points. We have too much talent in this league to total 23 points. NFL guys like Blanda, Parilli, Flores and great offensive coaches, too—Gillman, Stram and Saban—we have to showcase a wide-open offense."

"Patience, Bud, patience. At least, the attendance was decent."

"If that many people really paid Friday night," said glass-half-empty Adams. "I hear they gave away tickets like cold grits."

"Patience, Bud, patience"

———※———

That Saturday was homecoming day for the 1960 Texas Longhorns, and Austin's streets were mobbed with fans watching the parade. The crowds waved pennants and yelled "attaboys" to anyone they recognized going by. Cheerleaders dressed in red-and-blue shorts vaulted in unison while dozens of baton twirlers paraded up the packed street in front of the band.

This homecoming game pitted Texas against Texas Tech, a huge interstate rivalry. Inside the stadium, fans with painted faces screamed insanely for their beloved Longhorns. When the Texas band blared their fight song, not a soul sat. The entire crowd stood, hungry for every nuance of every play, determined not to miss a second of the action.

—∞—

Far from that delirious and devoted crowd, a few hundred bundled optimists scattered amidst the cold, empty seats of War Memorial Stadium on Sunday. Sitting on the bench, two Buffalo Bills players removed their helmets and looked up at the dismal turnout.

"You deposit your paycheck yet?" Billy Shaw asked. "Mine bounced yesterday."

"Bounced already?" Stew Barber rotated his neck and glanced upward.

"Look at the stands. No wonder the check bounced. They're gonna need to start playing these games in phone booths. We're lucky that they don't make us go up there and introduce ourselves."

—∞—

Lamar was on the phone to Bud Adams Monday, turning the pages of the morning newspaper.

"No, believe me. I did the stats, terrible attendance, every team, very disappointing. We've got to improve our product.... What do you think about this idea? What if we build star power by putting the names of the players on the backs of their jerseys?"

"Name recognition? That could be counterproductive," Adams said. "Once the public knows the player's names, they will want more money."

"Maybe, but it will be worth it if it creates fan interest. We only have one chance to build an audience and must pull out all the stops. Let's have the scoreboard clock keep the official time. If the fans know exactly how much time the quarterback has to score, that'll add tension. It'll enhance the excitement of late-game drives. Before long, we could even have cameras on rollers moving up and down the sidelines. That would make our product more marketable. Why limit networks to static 50 yard line shots?"

"I give you credit, Lamar," Adams said. "You're always thinking."

"Another thing I found interesting … of our total attendance, only 3,000 were colored."

"Three thousand? Shit, we only had about seventy negroes in Houston. Easy to spot; we sat them all in one segregated section."

"If you integrate seating, you'll draw a lot more colored fans. It works for us."

"You crazy, Lamar? Several NFL teams, including George Preston Marshall's Washington Redskins, don't have any colored players. The nation's capitol is still racist, and you want me to integrate the stands in Houston? Houston, Texas? When a colored suits up for the Redskins, then maybe I'll think about it."

"Before Dallas entered the league, the Redskins were the southernmost team in the NFL, so it might be more about the size of his purse than outright prejudice. Marshall is a good old West Virginia boy, though, so who knows?"

Lamar made a quick note in his yellow pad.

"But maybe you're right. Dallas might be farther from Houston than the geographical points would indicate. You might be shooting yourself in the foot with a bold move like integration and a new product. Whether to negroes or whites, we need to sell more tickets. We have to make ourselves more marketable." Lamar made another notation. "Well, here's a little good news that'll help. We're finally legitimate. The Vegas bookies are making odds on us. If the public can wager on us, it's gotta add interest."

"At least that's something…." Adam's said.

"Speaking about bookies, did you read about the latest mess Carroll Rosenbloom got himself into?"

Finding themselves on the front page was rare for a team owners, yet the *Baltimore Herald's* headline read "Rosenbloom Attorneys Deny He Bet Against Own Team." The *Baltimore Sun's* headline read "Four to Testify in Rosenbloom Betting Scandal."

—w—

In his office, a furious Rosenbloom and a concerned Art Modell listened through a speakerphone, as Pete Rozelle stuttered through the other end.

"The feds have four witnesses willing to swear in court that they placed bets for you, on and against the Colts, ranging from $500,000 to $1 million. They're testifying. It's going to get ugly."

"Shut the hell up and listen to me. You fix this. That's why we hired you. Fix it, or we'll get another commissioner. You'll be out of football on your ass."

"The wise guys won't like this Pete," Modell said. "Get it fixed. We don't need the feds poking around. Mr. Gambino called me this morning. He wants to know what the hell's going on. He said if we can't run our own shop, he'll run it for us."

"I know my job. I'll handle it," Rozelle said.

"Don't drag us down, Pete. The TV money's too good," Modell said. "I'm making more now than I ever did at the track or from the tote machines."

Carroll's lips compressed into a thin purple line, his eyes as hard as onyx.

"Fuck you, Modell. Don't drag 'us' down. I'm the one on the hook here, not you and not Carlos Gambino or any of his guinea hoods."

Carroll turned from Modell and yelled into the speaker at Rozelle.

"Go do what you have to, but you better make this thing disappear, or you're out on your ass. You understand me? Out on your ass!"

—w—

Rozelle didn't need Rosenbloom to remind him that his job was protecting the appearance of NFL integrity. A player gambling or an owner having Mafia associations didn't become a problem until the situation received publicity. Then it was Rozelle's job as commissioner to spin it.

It was cold and breezy that Monday morning when Rozelle read from a prepared statement. The week before had been profitable for the four witnesses after they had received subtle visits from two burly men in a black Lincoln. The Luca Brasi lookalikes delivered thick manila envelopes and stern warnings to all the witnesses.

Rosenbloom had done his job, and now it was Rozelle's turn to do his.

"After investigating the betting allegations against Carroll Rosenbloom, the commissioner finds them unsubstantiated," a nervous Rozelle said. "Especially since the three men involved have since rescinded their testimony."

A reporter yelled, "What were the witnesses' names, Commissioner?"

The ever-dapper Rozelle reached for a white pocket square from his Italian silk suit, dabbed it slowly across his forehead. Taking a deep breath before folding the pocket square carefully and placing it back in his top pocket, he abruptly said, "That's a moot point. The subject is now closed. Thank you, gentlemen."

Hours later at Belmont Park, New York, the racehorses galloped to the finish line as a waiter placed a phone at Rosenbloom's table. By this time, he and Georgia had become inseparable.

"Yeah, you handled it beautifully," Carroll said. "That 'the commissioner finds them unsubstantiated' was a nice touch. One thing. If there's a next time, remember, there were four men. You should have said all four men rescinded their testimony, not three."

With his left hand plastered against the glass of a telephone booth, a relieved Pete Rozelle heard Carroll's soothing words.

"You've proved your worth, for a while, anyway. Nice job." As the horses headed to the starting gate, Carroll heard the familiar bugle indicating first call.

"I've gotta go now. If nothing else comes up, don't call me until tomorrow morning. If anything breaks, no matter how small, call me immediately. Am I clear? Immediately. If I'm going to hear bad news, I want to hear it before my enemies hear it." Rosenbloom hung up and turned to Georgia.

"Remember that McLuhan fellow? You remember that night when we first met at Joe Kennedy's party? I'll never quite get that guy out of my head. He had it right. How did he put it? 'Perception creates reality?' 'The medium is the message?' He was damn right. Rozelle's little speech reeked of greasepaint and cardboard, but they bought it. With the proper PR, we can make John Q. Public believe anything."

CHAPTER TWENTY

The AFL played their first championship game on New Year's Day, 1961. The Houston Oilers led by quarterback George Blanda defeated the Los Angeles Chargers 24–16 at Houston's Jeppesen Field. Future Republican vice presidential candidate Jack Kemp quarterbacked the losers.

The next day, The Foolish Club met at Adams's office to await the ratings on ABC's hotline.

"One hell of a game, Bud, congratulations," said Buffalo's Ralph Wilson. "Other than Lamar, there's no more deserving guy to win the first AFL championship."

"Well, at least Lamar won the consolation prize." Adams's mouth bent into a wry grin. "That son of a bitch Abner Haynes sure as hell galloped away with player of the year. We will all have our day in the sun. Yesterday was mine."

Some of the press had latched on to The Loser's Club moniker, and Barron Hilton wasn't happy. After his eight point defeat the day before, Hilton was screaming for some solace.

"Where the hell are those ratings?"

"Patience, Barron, patience," Lamar counseled. He fiddled with some notes atop his desk for a few moments but soon gave up and looked straight at Adams. "Bud, go ahead and dial that hotline again."

"I just dialed five minutes ago." Adams laughed. "You're preaching patience and losing yours."

"What else do you have to do? The season's over," Lamar said.

Adams dialed the phone and listened a few seconds before letting out a big whoop.

"Yee haw, 44-freaking-million people watched that game. Imagine, 44 million?"

As members of The Foolish Club congratulated each other, a satisfied Lamar thought, Losers Club, huh? Wait till Pop hears these numbers.

—ɷ—

Just a few short weeks later in our nation's capital, something far more important happened. Joe Kennedy's dream had come true. Aristotle finally had his young Alexander. Our thirty-fifth president, a vibrant John F. Kennedy, delivered a poignant and prescient inaugural address.

"Let every nation know, whether it wishes us well or ill, that we shall pay any price, bear any burden, meet any hardship, support any friend, oppose any foe, to assure the survival and the success of liberty ... this much we pledge—and more."

Ultimately the price would include over 58,000 of our nation's bravest young men. The Best and the Brightest, as Kennedy's Cabinet came to be known, subscribed to the prevailing yet incorrect foreign policy theory held by the two previous administrations.

The domino theory was first proposed by Eisenhower after WWII as justification for US intervention in Turkey and Greece. The theory hypothesized that if one country in the region fell under communist influence, the surrounding countries would follow in a so-called domino effect.

Ike had applied that theory to Southeast Asia, Kennedy followed suit.

The real tragedy of Vietnam is that our invasion was never about Southeast Asia or even about communism.

The Soviet Premiere, Nikita Khrushchev's life, had been tempered by an upbringing of deprivation and strife. Additionally, Khrushchev had seen WWI up close and personal. In their first meeting, he held nothing but disdain for the young and privileged Kennedy. After a three-hour meeting with Khrushchev, Kennedy had exited the room and plopped into the first available bench. Sighing, he reached for his fedora and slid it down over his eyes.

A White House reporter asked, "Rough meeting, Mr. President?"

"About as rough as it gets," Kennedy said. Then, he leaped up and grabbed Kenny O'Donnell, his closest aide. "Where's it going on, right now?" he asked.

"Where's what going on right now, Mr. President?" O'Donnell asked.

"The communists. Where are they? Where can we make a stand?"

"Vietnam," O'Donnell said.

"Then, Vietnam it has to be. Khrushchev thinks that because I'm young that I'm soft. I can't allow that perception to stand."

Contrary to revisionist history, to win the Democratic nomination and later the election, Kennedy had to out-hawk all the Republican Party candidates on national defense. After China fell in 1948, the Republican mantra was that Truman and the Democrats were responsible for allowing Chairman Mao's revolution to succeed. "The Democrats lost China" refrain released any previous restrictions on acrid political discourse and helped Eisenhower beat Adlai Stephenson, ending the Democratic reign of the past twenty-two years.

Always with his ear to the ground and his hand on the pulse of the electorate, Kennedy was aware that oversimplification—today's bumper sticker wisdom—had enormous influence with the American people.

Whether he was or wasn't, Kennedy had to appear as a strong anti-communist to erase the perception that the Democratic Party was soft on defense. That hawkish approach and his father's money, coupled with his television charisma, had helped him squeak by the avid communist hunter Richard Nixon.

CHAPTER TWENTY-ONE

Although struggling at the box office, Lamar's Dallas Texans were still outdrawing the Cowboys, and several other AFL teams were almost breaking even. Meanwhile, Harry Wismer had been running the New York franchise like a Dollar Store. A sign over Wismer's open apartment door read "Titans' Business Office." A passerby strolled in off the street, dropped $10 on Harry's kitchen table, grabbed two tickets, and left. Down the hallway, the Titans coach drew plays on a child's blackboard set up in Harry's living room.

The entire operation had the stability of a floating crap game.

At the Polo Grounds, conditions were just as bad. The Titans' dismal locker room was littered with broken glass. On the mirrors above the sinks, encrusted shaving cream spelled out "Fuck You Harry" and "How about some hot water?"

Wismer was so broke that he couldn't even pay his electric bill. A Titans game finished in the dark, so Harry could save $250. The spectators squinted and could barely see each other, never mind the opaque field.

Titans players entered their parking lot to find their cars vandalized. Shattered windshields and flat tires speckled the upper Harlem facility. One player turned to another. "Wismer said he renovated this dump? If he did, he put lipstick on a corpse."

—◆—

On payday, Titans players queued up anxiously at the bank to cash their checks. They strained their necks, wondering if the tellers had any of Harry's money left. Things were so dismal that when the Titans played a road game in San Diego, players clutched their helmets and shoulder pads while hitchhiking dejectedly back to their hotel because Wismer hadn't paid for the Titans team bus.

—⁓—

One Sunday afternoon, a group of team members bunched behind Joe Foss inside their filthy locker room. Some players were sitting on milk crates and watching game films projected on a bedsheet. Foss had the phone to his ear.

"Thanks, Mr. Hunt. I knew you'd say that."

Foss hung up and turned to an angry gang of players.

"Boys, Mr. Hunt said you have his personal assurance that all your financial concerns will be met. Now go on out there and destroy the Raiders."

The final score read Raiders 44, Titans 10. After the game, a few Titan players climbed into the stands and introduced themselves to the sprinkle of spectators left after the debacle.

—⁓—

Harry Wismer's sad reality was he didn't have money for his facilities and didn't have money to sign drafted players to compete with the NFL. Despite his personal feelings for Wismer, Lamar was left with no choice but to search for an owner with enough money to compete.

—⁓—

Before the regular season began the following year, The Foolish Club sat around their conference table with Harry Wismer's absence blatantly obvious.

Barron Hilton leaned to his left and whispered to Ralph Wilson.

"When I open a hotel, I need land, bricks, and cement. For this venture, all I needed was capital. Now, Hunt has me short on that. What a salesman this guy is. I walk in here ready to chuck the entire project, and by the time he gets through plying me with statistics and optimism, I dump another $100,000."

"I know what you mean," Wilson said. "Every time we meet, I feel like I'm sticking my chin out for another wallop."

Lamar didn't hear them. He was busy swinging.

"To sign stars in the upcoming draft, we are going to need cash, but our biggest problem right now is that we have a weak link in New York."

"A weak link? Harry's incompetence will topple the league," Bud Adams blurted out. "I know you want to save him, Lamar, but in this case loyalty's a weakness. Harry said the Titans average 15,000 in attendance. If that's true, 10,000 of those people must be disguised as empty seats. Christ, every fan in the stadium has his own personal hot dog vendor."

"I'll never forget that Harry's idea to split the profits saved our bacon, but we've come too far to let one man sink us," Lamar said. "If I lose $2 million a year, I'm good for the next seventy-five years. The rest of you aren't as fortunate."

"You've got to cut him loose, Lamar. Harry's delusional," Hilton said. "You know what he did when my Chargers front office asked for promotional pictures of the Titans stars? He sent us 100 pictures of himself."

"I'll deal with Harry, boys. That said, this year, expenses will decrease, and attendance will increase. I'm telling you that in three years, we'll be in the black. I believe our league is here to stay."

"Well, that's what you say," Hilton said. "Maybe Harry is delusional, but I'm not. Last year, I lost almost $1 million. I'm not grabbing a large-enough share of the market. After this year's championship game, I'm moving from L.A. to San Diego, only fifteen miles north of the Mexican border. I can't go any farther south than that. Right after the '62 championship game, that's it. I'm gone. I've made up my mind."

"I thought I was flexible and prepared for anything, but this really throws a few thorns in the grits," Hunt said. "Heck, it looks like I'm moving to Kansas City. Barron said he's moving to San Diego. The Raiders and Denver are sold. Minnesota has fled the league, and we might have to scrap the New York market…."

"We can't fail in New York, or the whole league will collapse," Adams said. "Get rid of Harry."

"It breaks my heart, but right after this year's championship game, either Harry moves his team to Miami, or he sells."

—ɱ—

After the AFL '62 championship game, the back-page headline poking from a stack of newspapers on Lamar's desk offered a ray of hope: "AFL Born at the Age of Three."

With freight-train enthusiasm, Lamar raved to his ex-wife.

"Look at these headlines. 'Dallas Texans Beat Houston Oilers in Six Quarters' splattered all over the country's newspapers. Wait till Rosenbloom reads this. We've knocked the established league off the back pages. Double overtime, what a game. No one can say we're not entertainment now."

"I'm happy for you, Lamar, but you must put things in perspective," Rosemary said. "You're on an emotional roller coaster. First depression then elation. This is only a part of your life, not all of it. You're letting this project overwhelm you. I warned you. This league was a mistake."

"But the irony of it all. We won the championship by playing only the second overtime game in history. We have a hot young quarterback with Lenny Dawson, a great running back in Abner Haynes, and we have to leave Dallas? With that midget quarterback Eddie LeBaron, the Cowboys averaged 10 points less than us a game. Shoot, they're so dull that paint watches the Cowboys dry, yet they get to stay."

Lamar switched from manic to maudlin as he pondered the future.

"As great as this victory was, I don't think I had any other choice but to move the ball club. Leaving Texas will break my heart. It really will. That was the point of my entire odyssey. I just wanted to bring an NFL team to Dallas. Now, I find myself about to move to Kansas City with a whole new league."

"It's God's will. Accept the things you cannot change and change the things you can. Put your faith in the Lord, and things will work out for the best."

"The Lord's all well and good, Rosemary, and I'll need his help. But some things I can change. One thing that I learned when the Giants and the Dodgers left New York was that relocating to other cities gives a professional sports team leverage. I was able to negotiate a damn good agreement with the mayor of Kansas City for our stadium out at Arrowhead, a lot better than any deal I could have gotten in Dallas.

"Another thing I can control is the name of the new franchise. The mayor's name is H. Roe Bartle, but his nickname among the Boy Scouts is Chief. How do you feel about the Kansas City Chiefs?"

—m—

An eager reporter interviewed Lamar's quarterback Len Dawson later that week.

"Lenny, would you comment on the rumor that Mr. Hunt is moving the team to Kansas City?"

"Well, I don't have much to say about it. My contract doesn't specify where I play. It specifies who I play for."

"Is Mr. Hunt moving the club to Kansas City, Missouri, or Kansas City, Kansas?"

Dawson stopped signing autographs and stared at the reporter. "Wait a minute! There are two Kansas Cities?"

Lamar Hunt, founder of the Kansas City Chiefs, at Arrowhead Stadium, July 1, 1972. Public domain.

Oil magnate H.L. Hunt, Lamar's father. Public domain

Members of The Foolish Club, 1961. Seated, l-r are K.S. "Bud" Adams Jr. and Commissioner Joe Foss. Standing, l-r: Bill Sullivan, Carl Kunz, Ralph Wilson, Lamar Hunt, Harry Wismer, Wayne Valley, and Barron Hilton. Courtesy of the American Football League Hall of Fame, http://www.re-membertheafl.com.

Carroll Rosenbloom, owner of the Baltimore Colts, sits with First Lady Jacqueline Kennedy during the First Inaugural Salute to the President dinner commemorating the anniversary of President John F. Kennedy's inauguration, January 20, 1962. Photo by Abbie Rowe, White House Photographs, courtesy of the National Archives.

Georgia Frontiere, aka Mrs. Carroll Rosenbloom, December 6, 1969. Photo by Richard Gummere/ New York Post Archives/ (c) NYP Holdings, Inc. via Getty Images.

Al Davis, owner of the Oakland Raiders. Mitchell Haddad Photography.

Tim Mara (seated center left), owner of the New York Giants, at the Jamaica Race Track, 1934. Public domain.

Poor People's March at Lafayette Park and on Connecticut Avenue, Washington, D.C., June 18, 1968. Photo by Warren K. Leffler, courtesy Library of Congress.

Bert Bell, Commissioner of the National Football League (center) and George Marshall, owner of the Washington Redskins (right), present an annual pass to NFL games to President Harry Truman, September 15, 1949. Public domain.

Lyndon B. Johnson (center) receives a solid-gold lifetime pass to all NFL games, June 7, 1967. Also pictured from left are Edward Bennett Williams, President of the Washington Redskins; Senator Everett Dirksen; NFL Commissioner Pete Rozelle; and Congressman Gerald Ford. The gentleman at the far right is unidentified. Photo courtesy of the National Archives.

Medal of Honor winner and WWII flying ace Captain Joe Foss, USMC, ca. 1942-43. He would later serve as the governor of South Dakota before serving as the first Commissioner of the newly created American Football League from 1959-1966. United States Marine Corps photo, http://hqine001.hqmc. usmc.mil/HD/IMAGES/ MOH/World_War_II/ Hi_Res/Foss_JJ.jpt

Joe Namath in 1965, featured in Jet Stream *magazine. Public domain.*

In New York City, the cab driver could sit at the bar next to Mickey Mantle at Toots Shor's establishment. Pictured l-r: Frank Sinatra, Toots Shor, Rocky Marciano, and Joe DiMaggio. Public domain.

New York Titan's owner Harry Wismer, December 1961. Public domain.

Sportscaster Howard Cosell. He "told it like it was" and was an early supporter of the upstart AFL. Public domain.

CHAPTER TWENTY-TWO

T he average citizen felt our institutions were falling apart. Football was no different. Pete Rozelle had gathered information about a possible betting scandal involving two of the NFLs brightest stars, Alex Karras and Paul Hornung. He told the league's owners about it, and they discussed the dilemma.

"What have you got on these two sons of bitches, Pete?" Carroll asked. "How much did they bet and how often?"

"Hornung bet up to $500 at least a half dozen times, and Karras bet even less, somewhere between $50 and $100. Insignificant amounts, really, but if the public perceives our product as impure, the consequences could be dire and insurmountable. The fans can't think that players could actually benefit from not trying their best."

"Pete's right," Rooney said. "We can't have a watered-down product. Fans must know that every lad is trying his best at all times."

"If the public knew that we bet, that would be bad enough," Modell said. "But if they think we permitted the players to gamble, we're dead. Come down hard on them, Pete. Address it now and with authority. This scandal could spread like a virus."

"Then I have your permission to suspend them? I feel we should make it indefinitely. I can always show leniency later, but for now, our image must be zero tolerance."

Carroll had been silent up to now, but his firm voice made it unanimous.

"It could become a plague. There is no room for debate here. We can't have this gambling thing spread."

"Ah ... sure. Art and Carroll are right," Rooney said. "Do it dramatically, Pete. Make an indelible statement. Our league won't abide gambling. Now if we're done here, I'll be running along. Post time in an hour. I have a small interest in the first race."

—ᴍ—

After the commissioner handed down the two suspensions, America's most influential sportscaster made it his opening story.

"This is Howard Cosell speaking of sports. Pete Rozelle faced his biggest challenge as commissioner yesterday. He became aware of a gambling scandal, which tore at the very fabric of the league that he swore to defend. He acted swiftly and without mercy.

"Two of the league's biggest stars were suspended indefinitely. Paul Hornung and Alex Karras will not play professional football this season and may never play again. In this reporter's opinion, Rozelle did the right thing. Indeed, his actions have met with approval from owners, fans, and sportswriters alike. Even Hornung's coach, Vince Lombardi, approved. Today, once and for all, Rozelle gained everybody's complete respect. He showed that he's a commissioner that won't be trifled with, a commissioner tough on gambling."

—ᴍ—

A cynical reporter heard Cosell's broadcast and laughed with his friend at the Washington Post. "Yeah, Rozelle came down hard on the players. What does he do when the owners get caught gambling?"

His companion smirked. "Don't tell me that Rozelle isn't neutral. The owners pay him a small fortune to be neutral."

CHAPTER TWENTY-THREE

Late spring of 1963 saw a nation in turmoil. Many Americans were for the war, some against it, still others indifferent. Our electorate was polarized. With this spirit of change and rebellion, a visionary came along and saw potential in the New York Titans where everyone else saw only disaster.

David Abraham "Sonny" Werblin had made a career identifying and managing talent. His list of clients was a "Who's Who" in music television and movies. He was the CEO of the Music Corporation of America (MCA), a group of agents so powerful that jealous competitors once joked that pneumonia was merely a cold represented by MCA.

Werblin was the right man at the right time.

He had tenacity, comprehension, and clout. His favorable connections with NBC later proved invaluable when the new league had to negotiate TV deals. As a man with connections, it was no surprise that he would assemble his potential investors to meet at the famous Broadway watering hole, Toots Shor's.

Toots Shor's wasn't just a bar. It was an institution where all classes of people rubbed elbows and tilted pilsner glasses democratically. A mailman might find himself on a stool next to Yankees superstar Mickey Mantle or writer Pete Hamill. It was Hamill who famously said about the restaurant, "Toots' was a part of the imagination of people who had never even been there. They knew it existed the way they knew the Statue of Liberty existed."

In the '40s, the entire restaurant stood and applauded as Toots promenaded in with Frank Sinatra, Babe Ruth, Jack Dempsey, and Bing Crosby. The four sultans of mid-century America strolled through the adoring crowd and made their way to a private table. If you were a celebrity in New York from the '40s to the '60s, Toots Shor's was the place to be. Sports icons, journalists, actors, mobsters, and politicians all lifted their glasses in the same smoke-filled room and not for the cuisine, which was described as "nuttin' fancy." It was to be insulted by the man himself.

Shor was a gruff barrel of a man who had grown up in South Philly and made his appearance on the New York scene as a bouncer at the Five O'clock Club, his first introduction to celebrities. He adored taunting stars with quick one-liners to let them know that, to him, they were all just mugs. One afternoon, Frank Sinatra was surrounded by adoring fans. Toots pushed through the crowd, handed the icon a $5 bill, and said, "Here, kid. Run next door and get me some coffee."

One might see Toots consorting with Chief Justice Earl Warren one moment and hobnobbing with Mob boss Frank Costello the next. Shor insulted everybody equally. A testament to his diversity was that his New York City landmark at West 51st Street, a one-minute walk from Radio City Music Hall, was paid for with Jimmy Hoffa's Teamster pension funds, and the groundbreaking ceremony for his newer place at West 52nd Street was done by a Supreme Court Justice who even posed for a photo with the obligatory shovel of dirt.

Sonny Werblin spoke to a table full of big shots over lunch at Shor's and tried to sell them his vision for the Titans.

"That AFL championship game proved that this new league is viable entertainment, but their New York franchise is pitiful," Werblin said. "If Harry Wismer promised every fan a $100, he couldn't sell out the Polo Grounds. It's a long way from the hallowed grounds that Willie Mays once roamed. He's living in the past. It's a cesspool, and the neighborhood's a slum, strictly a second-class operation. He doesn't know what the hell he's doing. Hunt told me that we can steal the Titans for $1 million."

If the always impeccably dressed Werblin knew one thing, he knew entertainment. The double overtime game in Dallas had convinced him that football was pure show business. Gamblers by nature, Werblin's four potential investors were also his partners in his ownership of Monmouth Racetrack in New Jersey. The former agent spoke in no-nonsense, staccato sentences.

"Gentlemen, here we are in 1963, and the World's Fair opens in Flushing Meadows Park next year. Shea Stadium hosts baseball's New York Mets, and it needs a fall tenant. I say it should be us."

He gulped from a large glass of water while another potential stakeholder offered his thoughts.

"The Giants were blacked out yesterday, so I watched the Titans," Phil Iselin said. "I wonder how many other people did the same. It's a different brand of football ... wide open. No three yards and a cloud of dust ... impressive. It's like watching basketball in cleats." With the soft authoritative voice of a CEO, Iselin made his case. "The NFL opened its door, and the AFL walked right in. If that door is still open, I agree with Sonny. I think we should too."

The next man to speak was medium height, his white hair slicked back atop an oversized forehead.

"You think football fans will travel all the way out to Queens?" Leon Hess asked.

"Give them a first-rate product and a safe place to watch it," Werblin snapped. "They'll go all right." He paused to tear the crust from a piece of Italian bread. "They call their baseball team out in Flushing 'the Mets.' We'll call our team 'the Jets.' The stadium is out near the airport, so it'll fit. Shit, it even rhymes with Mets. You want people to pay money? Put a star on the stage, someone who draws. Then give him a decent arena to perform in. Fans will come.'"

"I don't know. We'll have a lot to compete against," Hess said. "Giant fans are loyal, lifelong.-"

"Think about what you just said, Leon—'lifelong.' The Giants are old," Sonny barked. "The country is changing. Young people are restless. They want antiheroes, not heroes. Even their signs say don't trust anyone over the age of thirty. They don't trust the establishment, fine? We'll offer them the alternative that they want. They'll come all right, and we'll profit from it."

—m—

The new owners meant what they said about a first-rate product. They transformed the once dilapidated Titan locker room into a spotless facility. Sonny Werblin spoke in front of the assembled players.

"You're now a member of the New York Jets organization," Werblin said. "Next year we will be moving into a new stadium out in Queens. This is your new coach Weeb Ewbank. Your new uniforms are Kelly green and white. Everything around here will be new. New. You hear me? Everything, including your attitudes." Momentarily distracted from his prepared speech, he paused and pointed.

"Wait a minute. What's that man doing?"

A trainer taping a pair of cracked shoulder pads looked up.

"Who me? I'm fixing these pads, Mr. Werblin."

"Throw those pads away. You hear me? Throw them away and get new ones. I want everything around here first-class. Now that we've gotten that straight, Coach Ewbank wants to say a few words. Weeb?"

"Gentlemen, Mr. Werblin has made a financial and emotional commitment to this franchise. Besides the obvious cosmetic changes to this organization, he has assured me he will do his utmost to pursue talent, not just player talent but talent throughout the front office and with our coaches. He has brought me in to pursue the five-year plan that helped me build the Baltimore Colts into world champions. I told him I could do the same with the Jets, and he has taken me at my word. This locker room has sixty-five bodies but only a few football players. That is going to change, and I mean fast." The avuncular man, with a hefty paunch, spoke intently. "This is a new dawn, gentleman. When you play for me, you'll work as hard as you can, or you'll be gone. If you're not ready to give 120 percent, pack now. When you fly with the New York Jets, you'll fly first class, or you won't fly at all."

CHAPTER TWENTY-FOUR

B y the fall of '63, Georgia had moved in with Carroll. She sat
stunned on their sofa as the conscience of American broadcast journalism interrupted the soap opera *As the World Turns*
to deliver a heartbreaking news flash at 1:40 p.m. Eastern time.

"This is Walter Cronkite in the CBS newsroom. We interrupt
this program to deliver a news bulletin. Three shots have been
fired at President Kennedy's motorcade in downtown Dallas.
The first reports say that President Kennedy has been seriously
wounded by the shooting." That was all that was broadcast, nothing more, no speculation, no talking heads. Then CBS switched
back to their soap opera but not for long.

With Cronkite now behind his desk, CBS switched back to
the tragedy. Almost one hour after their initial news bulletin, he
said, "From Dallas, Texas, this flash, apparently official, President
Kennedy died at 1 p.m., Central Standard Time." He removed his
glasses and glanced at the classroom-like clock clinging to the
wall. "Two o'clock, Eastern Standard Time, approximately some
thirty-eight minutes ago." After replacing his glasses, Cronkite
choked up, hesitated a few moments, his upper lip biting the lower before trying to continue as professionally as possible. "Vice
President Johnson has left the hospital...."

Georgia dashed to dial Carroll at his office.

"Have you seen the news?"

"I have it on right now, heartbreaking. His poor family and
those two young children."

"I still can't believe it. Who would do such a thing?"

"Powerful men make powerful enemies, none more so than the President of the United States."

"This has to be the act of a madman."

"Maybe, maybe not," Carroll said. "Kennedy and his old man had many influential enemies. Remember how Joe double-crossed the Mob in West Virginia? Hell, without Sam Giancana's help with the unions, the kid never wins the election. H.L. Hunt ran full-page ads in Dallas all last week accusing Kennedy of being a communist. I hope this tragedy paints a big cloud over Hunt and his whole family."

—⟶⟵—

The young president's death placed the entire country in mourning. Much of the power that the Kennedy name would exert over the national imagination in the decades to follow would be a direct result of that ghastly day in Dallas.

Although the world's grief and shock were genuine, they were not entirely for the dead president himself. TV had made Jack Kennedy a figure larger-than-life, so young, so vibrant, a beautiful wife and fabulous kids. Yet he was the first American president to die at the hands of an assassin since President McKinley sixty-two years prior. Even those who didn't agree with him were shook by the brazenness of his death. It rattled the confidence of the American people that we couldn't even keep our president safe. Television, the medium that got him elected, was now the medium that ironically documented his murder.

The president's death and its perceived cover-up by the Warren Commission (real or imagined), the continuing lies surrounding the Vietnam War, the My Lai Massacre and the Pentagon Papers, all combined to exponentially increase the average voter's distrust of government.

The public began questioning the wholesome image of our government and began to think that maybe, just maybe, they were being manipulated.

The spreading skepticism spilled out onto the people's podium, the streets.

In the weeks to come, black mobs overturned cars and set fires to buildings in Memphis and elsewhere. Rampaging blacks in Tennessee threw bricks through store windows chanting, "No justice, no peace."

Others found solace by protesting for peaceful change. Beneath the shadow of the Lincoln Memorial, a nonviolent assembly of 250,000 people gathered to listen to Martin Luther King's "I Have a Dream" speech.

CHAPTER TWENTY-FIVE

The Vietnam War had overshadowed all LBJ's domestic achievements, his war on poverty, the Civil Rights Act, and all other aspects of his Great Society. Kennedy had accomplished little in his 1,000-day tenure. The Republican Congress had blocked most of his initiatives and had shot down the Civil Rights Act years earlier on a states' rights basis because of a clause in the bill, which made it a federal crime to lynch Negroes.

The Southern Senators had argued that lynching blacks should be a state-by-state decision. This unimaginable indignity came more than a decade after many blacks had died "for freedom" in WWII.

Johnson knew how to wield the power of the Senate like no president past or present, having learned it at the knee of Richard Russell, a fervent racist who would have been president if not for Jim Crow. LBJ used that knowledge and the goodwill created by Kennedy's assassination to push through his administration's massive civil rights legislation.

Despite his domestic achievements, the unpopular war and the even more unpopular draft were insurmountable problems for LBJ. Weary citizens watched on nightly newsreels as their soldiers trudged through jungles in a country that most had never even heard of only a decade before. They saw the elephant grass swirling and denting from the blades of Jolly Green Giant helicopters painted with shark's teeth. Boys who had only last season played American Legion Baseball were staining that tall green grass with bright red blood, and the electorate was sick of it.

—ww—

Thousands of hippies smothered the White House lawn. The odor of marijuana blanketed the area with a strong pungent fog. In various stages of undress, protesters waved signs: "LSD melts in your mind and not in your hand" and "War is not healthy for children and other living things."

One ostentatious couple copulated below a poster that read "Make Love Not War." Some burned draft cards under signs that read "Drop acid not bombs" and "Diem was a sonofabitch."

From his oval office window, President Lyndon Johnson stared down at the packs of protesters and heard them shouting, "Hey, hey, LBJ, how many kids have you killed today?"

LBJ pointed his chin at the demonstrators before turning to his Secretary of Defense, Robert McNamara.

"Look at all those people. They all hate the war. Well, who doesn't? I inherited this war from you and the rest of your smart Ivy League boys."

"The generals assure me if we bomb North Vietnam, we can win." McNamara said

LBJ turned quickly back to the window and sneered.

"I've heard that from you and the joint chiefs before, and I've heard it from your so-called best and brightest too. Now, I've got Bobby Kennedy up my ass even though it was his brother that got me into this mess."

Johnson backed away from the window, lowered his bottom lip, grimly bit the upper, and massaged his temples.

"After I sign that Civil Rights Act, Democrats will lose elections in the South, but if I lose this war, Democrats will lose the whole country."

CHAPTER TWENTY-SIX

The two executives in charge of ABC Sports, Edgar Scherick and Tom Moore, discussed the AFL's upcoming 1965 contract over the din of deafening dance music. Four strippers sliding and writhing on brass poles appeared and disappeared beneath sharp purple and bright blue strobe lights. Scherick hoisted a Heineken, leaned close to Moore's ear, and hollered.

"I read a sports opinion piece yesterday. It said that the AFL stood for the 'All Fun League' and the NFL for the 'No Fun League.'"

"Well, the AFL is wide open and makes for damn good theater. That five-year contract we signed with them worked out better than we could have ever imagined, but it expires this year," Moore yelled. "Maybe we should re-sign them early?"

"Offer them $600,000 per team. The other league is still the real prize. Did you know that NFL agreements say that nothing restricts us from televising Sunday doubleheaders? If we show East Coast games at 1 p.m., then switch to the West Coast for 4 p.m. games, imagine the financial possibilities. That's the brass ring, and that's why the upcoming bids for the old league's contract is key. We have to win that bid."

Inside the headquarters of The Foolish Club the following week, a crucial discussion was taking place.

"ABC just offered us $600,000 per team," Hilton said. "That's $24 million for five years. We should take it."

"Barron, Sonny here negotiates for Frank Sinatra, Bob Hope, Elizabeth Taylor, and Johnny Carson," Lamar said. "Don't you think we should take a back seat here?" He turned to Werblin. "The bigger the gap between the two contracts, the less legitimate we look. Our numbers must be close to theirs, Sonny. Do you think you can pull that off?"

"Leave this to me. First off, we're refusing that first offer. I'm not even using it as a starting point. We won't negotiate from there. Trust me, fellas. I'm not going to leave a single dollar on the table."

—∞—

Martinis in hand, Carroll and Georgia sat on their screen porch and stared out at an idyllic Florida bay.

"Rozelle announces who gets that new television contract in two days," Carroll said.

"You expect a bidding war?" Georgia asked.

"You think I'd leave something as critical as that to chance? It cost me $50,000, but I know the amount that ABC will be bidding. I've also figured out how to get CBS to inflate their bid."

"That's my guy, always ahead of the pack. Your partners are lucky."

"Partners? How much have you had to drink? I already made the arrangements to buy them out. Those guys have no idea how big this contract will be. I'm not sharing this money."

"But you said the announcement is in two days?"

"I bought them out last month. They're not stupid. It cost me a fortune, but they're clueless about this contract. Our league just okayed Sunday doubleheaders."

"I should have known." Georgia hoisted her cocktail and slurred sloppily. "Here's to the sole owner of the Baltimore Colts."

"You have a pretty good head start on me with that gin. Slow down. I can't stand it when you're sloshed."

Georgia glared icily but said nothing. She knew something about drunks. She also knew something that Carroll didn't. Those who shoot for the stars sometimes start in the gutter. She stared into her drink and drifted to a nightclub in Fresno, California, in

1940. On a garbage-strewn street, cars were parked in front of a seedy nightclub. The marquee read "The Singing Pamela Sisters."

—m—

Georgia and her mother, Lucia, performed in front of a small, squalid audience. They crooned "Don't Sit Under the Apple Tree," adjacent to an A-frame displaying the band's name. As Georgia left the stage, a slovenly drunk accosted her.

"Hey, baby, sit down here and have a drink. Come on, let's have a party."

A hardened teenager, Georgia pushed the man away with disgust.

Then, Georgia's mind raced ahead to the summer of 1942 when she escaped all of that. That day she threw her clothes into a suitcase and argued with Lucia.

"You can't stop this marriage. Frank loves me. I've had enough of this life. Booking me, your fifteen-year-old daughter, as your sister? No way I'll end up like you. I want a better life, and I'll do what it takes. I'm going places … starting tonight."

"Marry Frank? Are you crazy? Learn from me. You don't want a husband. To men, women are anchors. They'll use you and then cast you aside. Listen to me. You don't know anything. You're just a kid."

"I'm done listening to you and everyone else. From now on, no one controls my life."

Georgia stormed out with her suitcase and slammed the door.

"You'll never be anything without me!" Lucia screamed. "You need me."

Georgia leaped into Frank's car. As the car peeled away, Georgia's beat-up teddy bear rested on the back seat next to her suitcase, a helpless, inanimate observer of a desperate decision that would pave Georgia's future.

CHAPTER TWENTY-SEVEN

C lad in a swimsuit, with a towel tossed casually over his shoulder, Carroll phoned Rozelle from his Florida home.

"Pete, here's how we're gonna handle this bid tomorrow. Call Bill McPhail at CBS. Tell him that you got wind that NBC has a higher bid. Tell him you don't want NBC to win the contract, so it would be smart for him to up his bid. Call me back in an hour and a half. I've got to swim some laps."

The following day, behind a lectern at NFL headquarters, Pete Rozelle began to open the three sealed envelopes that would award the NFL's television contract for the next two years. He lifted the first, so the reporters could see it.

"Our first bid is from ABC."

Stern and businesslike, Rozelle tore open the envelope.

"ABC bids $26 million."

Oohs and ahhs spewed from the spectators.

"The next bid is from NBC," Pete said.

Because NBC's Carl Lindeman was the only television executive unaware that the NFL now had permission to broadcast doubleheaders, his bid was embarrassingly low.

Rozelle tore open the envelope … and fastened on Lindeman.

"NBC bids $20 million."

This brought a series of groans.

"CBS has the evening's final bid."

Tension mounted. Rozelle reached for the final envelope and tore it open.

"Congratulations, CBS — $28 million. The NFL looks forward to our continued partnership with the Columbia Broadcasting Network. Thank you, gentlemen, for your courtesy and for your continued support of professional football."

Rozelle turned and walked off the lectern while the winning bid elicited predictable applause from newsmen and spectators. A devastated Carl Lindeman shook his head and stared at the floor. His quivering right hand spread through a scalp wreathed with thinning hair. Lack of preparation had likely cost him his job at NBC.

At the eastern end of Spanish Key, a mass of herons, pelicans, avocets, sandpipers, egrets, and flamingos were building their nests or fishing in the shallows of the water. No televisions were available on the Florida island where Art Modell was vacationing. Art wore traditional mid-life Florida summer sandals, black socks, and white shorts, topped with a red-parrot-blotched shirt. He was understandably anxious to know the terms of the new television contract, so he hurried to the manager's office to answer Pete Rozelle's phone call.

"How did it go, Pete? What were the terms?"

"We got $14.1 million."

"Well I was hoping for more, but, hell, Pete, $7 million a year isn't exactly a stick in the eye. We can make it."

"No. Art, $14 million for one year, $28 million for two years."

Modell took the phone from his ear and stared puzzled into the receiver. "Stop with the bullshit, Pete. Maybe you better think about knocking off the Bloody Marys at breakfast."

Still the head of NBC sports for the moment, Lindeman returned to his office with a queasy stomach. A note on his desk read, "Please call AFL Commissioner Joe Foss." Lindeman's face flashed a ray of hope. His heart fluttered to his throat. Racing to the phone, he held his breath and dialed. Less than a week later, NBC and the AFL had a deal.

—⚬—

At a cold, windy Monday morning press conference in 1964, the AFL commissioner spoke.

"This $42 million partnership with NBC is the best thing that could have happened to us," Joe Foss said. "This five-year-contract is nine times the amount ABC signed with us only four years ago, and it will allow our teams to compete for high college draft choices. In short gentlemen, the American Football League is here to stay."

Amidst the flash of bulbs and a barrage of questions, a crowd of reporters scratched Foss's every word on long, thin pads.

—⚬—

The air outside the hospital window the Thursday morning after Foss's announcement was cool. The eastern sky was blue-colored and striped with low hanging red clouds. Wearing a cream-colored linen suit, a dark blue shirt, and blue suede shoes, Lamar lowered the hospital shade and twisted the venetian blinds before turning to the sound of his father's voice.

"Well, after that television contract," H.L. said. "You certainly don't have to call them mister anymore."

The beaming Lamar returned to a small, leather lounge chair next to his dad's bed. "Television has changed more than our league. It's changed everything. The long-term effects of this new medium won't be known for many decades."

The smile left his lips when he expressed a son's concern.

"But no need for us to discuss that now. The important thing now is for you to get some rest and for your tests to come back negative."

He rose and turned the bed's crank counterclockwise, winding it down to a sleeping position.

"I've got to return to my office, Dad. Now that the opportunists smell money, the demands on me are growing more every day. Apparently, everyone loves a winner."

"Do me a favor on your way out," H.L. said. "Stop on the third floor. There are Vietnam vets in that ward that don't get many visitors. A visit from you would mean a lot."

"Me? Why me? You should do it. You're the richest man in the world."

"True. But they love winners, too, and I don't own the Kansas City Chiefs."

Lamar sucked up the praise like a thirsty plant.

CHAPTER TWENTY-EIGHT

T he evening's Dallas sun had barely set in the west, yet the blue and white spotlights of Longhorn Country Club were already illuminating the circular fountain in the center of its huge lake. Lamar had recently remarried a woman who shared his priorities. Norma was both a churchgoing Baptist and an avid football and soccer fan. She loved the Lord, Lamar, and her fellow man, in that order. Although born in Arkansas, she appeared all Texan. Norma wore the blonde hair atop her petite body in a shoulder-length bob.

"What a week it's been, honey," Lamar said. "You should have seen Pop's face. Everyone in America now knows that my league is here to stay."

She sipped wine from a crystal glass and spread a white linen napkin across her lap, while Lamar adjusted his pricey gray silk tie, a nice compliment to his beige suit and sunburned shoes.

"Everything you worked and prayed for," Norma said. "It has all come to pass."

"Funny, all I wanted was a pro football team in Dallas. Instead, I create a whole new league and end up in Kansas City. Television has made this sport even bigger than baseball. Football and television need each other, just like we need each other, honey."

Norma lifted her wine to smiling lips.

"I can't believe how fortunate we were to find each other, Lamar. You complete me. I'm so happy."

She sipped her wine and looked out the picture window toward the fountain.

"You, Bud, Barron and all of The Foolish Club members are pioneers in a way."

"Yeah, I guess we are at that. Thank God I have you to share this moment with. What a day. I asked for an NFL franchise, and they shut me out. Well, now, I want more. God forgive me for being greedy, but I want one of our teams to beat one of theirs so badly...."

She gave her husband a curious look.

"One miracle in a lifetime should be enough. Savor this. Enjoy it. Don't tempt the Lord's patience."

"The Lord has nothing to do with it. Football embodies the tumultuous times we live in. Terms like bombs, bullet passes, sudden death—, those are the words of war. People are conditioned to pay attention to rhetoric with connotations of chaos and rage."

"I can't believe that sentence came out of your mouth. 'The Lord has nothing to do with it'? The Lord has everything to do with everything, including us finding each other. Like I said, savor the moment. Savor it the way I savor every moment with you."

♥

CHAPTER TWENTY-NINE

Around a large mahogany table, Sonny Werblin met again with the new Jets owners, enjoying drinks and conversation in a roped-off section of Toots Shor's.

"It's like when Joe DiMaggio walks into a room," Sonny said. "I can't explain it, but there's no doubt that this kid has it."

"Namath seems like he's throwing downhill, the fastest release I've ever seen," Weeb Ewbank said. "But his knees scare me, Sonny. I'm afraid if we sign him, he'll never play. I've seen them come and go. These kids can be great in college and never make it at our level. There's no guarantee, but I've got to admit this kid does seem special."

"Damn it, he's exciting. When he steps back and spirals those long passes," Sonny said, "I guarantee you he'll be as important to our league as Red Grange was to theirs. People will knock down doors to see this kid. He's a winner, and he'll make a winner of the Jets. I've been in show business thirty-three years. You put the stars of the stage out front. In football, quarterbacks are the bandleaders."

"Sonny has something there. Namath's handsome, with long hair, a real drugstore cowboy," Phil Iselin said before turning to Leon Hess. "Have you seen him, Leon? He looks like the type of guy who would hold up a 7–Eleven, slouched shoulders and a wise guy attitude, but when he throws—man, oh man—whoosh."

"These kids are screaming, 'Don't trust anyone over thirty,'" Werblin said. "I'm telling you. Namath's a natural for them."

"He's young, hip, and an antihero," Iselin said. "It's a chance for us to nurture a whole new fan base. I say damn the cost. I agree with Sonny. We go for Namath. He's the Cassius Clay of football."

—w—

After a sparring session the next morning in Louisville, newly crowned heavyweight boxing champion Cassius Clay grabbed a microphone. Perhaps the most idolized, vilified, and controversial figure of the twentieth century, reporters hung on his every word. His bold, brown, smooth face announced to the world his conversion to Islam.

"I hereby renounce my slave name Cassius Clay. From now on, I will be known as Muhammad Ali. Like my friend and brother Malcolm X, I am converting to the Nation of Islam, where I'll join the honorable Elijah Muhammad."

A tall, brash, lightning-quick boxer with a big mouth, Ali became a target for the right wing. He was outspoken on every social issue, from poverty to racism to, finally, his opposition to the Vietnam War. Old white America wondered why he couldn't be more like Joe Louis: just shut his mouth and do public relations tours for the Army.

Many of them would pay their hard-earned dough hoping to watch someone, anyone, black or white, who would just shut his big mouth.

—w—

Muhammed Ali inside the ring and Muhammed Ali outside the ring were two different people. Outside the ring, his abrasiveness, magnetic fearlessness, and infectious self-love electrified the world but also distracted people from his sniper's precision inside the ring. He was a heavyweight with the fluttering grace of a lightweight. He did everything you're not supposed to do when learning the art of boxing. He dropped his hands, seldom kept his left up, and even threw punches while backing up. He broke all the rules yet beat all the odds. He was that good.

In those years, boxing's heavyweight championship was the most coveted title in sports. Everyone knew who the heavyweight champ was, whether he was Ali, Rocky Marciano, or even Ingemar Johansson. Ali's title had made him the most identifiable face on the planet, more recognizable than President Johnson, or the majority of his predecessors. Hell, even the Beatles knew the value of having their picture taken with Ali.

Other black celebrities, like Sam Cooke or Marvin Gaye, were outspoken about civil rights and the war, but they felt they had to temper their sentiments due to the inevitable economic backlash. The heavyweight champion had no such reservations. With Ali in the lead, other black sports celebrities, including football's Jim Brown and basketball's Bill Russell and Lew Alcindor, felt inspired to speak out about the inequities of society. This opened the door for John Carlos and Tommie Smith to make their legendary closed-fist protest on the victory stand in the 1968 Olympics.

Ali's bluntness synergized with that unprecedented notoriety naturally made him a lightning rod for controversy. The only way to publicly silence Muhammed Ali was to beat him, and believe me, for most of white America, that could not happen soon enough.

CHAPTER THIRTY

Sonny Werblin looked out the portal window of a late afternoon American Airlines first-class flight to Miami. His eyebrows furrowed and his mouth tightened into a scowl before turning to Lamar.

"I'll feel a lot better when this kid's signature is on that contract."

"He's not scheduled to play tonight. Namath said he'd sign, so I don't see a problem."

"Yeah, but we need this guy bad. He's so damn important that I'll just feel better about everything after he's signed."

How bad is his knee?" Lamar asked.

"Coach Bryant said he re-hurt it during practice. Tragic that injury. Before the second quarter of that North Carolina game, the kid moved like a cat. He could really scramble. Did you know that Namath was a four-sport All-American in high school?"

"No. I didn't, but it's obvious to anyone who has ever watched a football game that a kid like this comes along once in a generation," Lamar said. "The Orange Bowl is in prime time tonight. If Namath plays, the whole nation will see him. That will make him even more valuable.... But if he plays and gets reinjured...."

—m—

Hours later, the great aircraft slowly bounded onto the Miami tarmac and taxied down the runway. When the two AFL owners disembarked, the dense rain clouds awaiting seemed like palls of pessimism. Their limousine was barely visible through the gloom.

—∿—

Ironically, Lamar and Sonny hadn't been the only ones financially concerned with the condition of Namath's knee that New Year's night. Bidwell's St. Louis Cardinals had selected the iconic quarterback with the twelfth pick of the NFL draft. When meeting with the Cardinal executives, Namath had demanded $200,000 and a new Lincoln Continental. While initially balking at Broadway Joe's requests, the Cardinals told Namath they would agree but only if he would sign before the Orange Bowl, which would have made him ineligible to play. Fierce competitor that he was, Namath declined. Fans who paid to witness that night's game, the millions who watched it on television, and, indeed, history itself would be forever grateful.

—∿—

It was stormy that New Years' night when Alabama played Texas for the 1965 national championship. The sold-out Orange Bowl was awash with mud, so disappointed fans didn't get to see the charismatic Namath start the game. Because of concern for his knee and the sloppy field, Bear Bryant didn't let Joe make his national television debut until just before halftime.

Two of America's renowned broadcasters Jim Simpson and Bud Wilkinson called this first-ever, nighttime telecast of an Orange Bowl.

"After the time-out, this next play will decide the ball game, Jim. Regardless of what happens on this last play, the nation has witnessed one of the finest bowl games ever played. To recap, when Texas jumped out to that early two-touchdown lead, they looked like they'd blow Alabama all the way back to Tuscaloosa."

"I think Bear Bryant was right not to start Namath, Bud. This young man has a fine future ahead of him. If number-one Alabama could handle number-six Texas without him, why risk his career?"

"I have to agree with you, Jim, but with ten minutes left in the half, and Alabama still scoreless, Bear Bryant had apparently seen enough. Despite Namath's injury, he had to put his prized quarterback into the game."

"A tough call for Bryant but let's remember what's at stake, Bud. This game will decide the national championship. Now, in the final seconds of the fourth quarter, Joe finally has a chance to be a hero."

"As our viewers know, Jim, when Bryant let Namath play shortly before the half, Alabama was down 14–0. He responded with a fourteen-play, ninety-seven-yard drive that finally put the Crimson Tide on the board and brought these Alabama fans to their feet."

"But this Texas team under Darryl Royal came right back, Bud. The Longhorns headed into the locker room at the half up 21–7."

"Let's give some credit to that Crimson Tide defense, Jim. They held Texas scoreless the entire second half while Namath was able to put 10 more points on the board. That brings us right up to date. Only seconds left with the score 21–17 and the national championship on the line. The tension in this stadium is palpable. Here we go with Alabama facing a fourth down on the Texas 1 inch line. Let me turn it over to you, Jim."

"Thanks, Bud. As we witnessed, Namath handed off to his fullback Steve Bowman three times, and three straight times the gallant Longhorn defense held. It's down to this last play for all the marbles ... the national championship."

Jim grinned into his microphone in anticipation and shouted, "Namath lines up over center and barks the signals. Here's the snap. Namath keeps it. It's a quarterback sneak. Wow, it's really close, Bud. I don't think he made it. No, he didn't make it. The Longhorns have held, and Texas wins the national championship. Whatta game. Whatta finish. Alabama loses a heartbreaker."

—∽∽—

Despite being named MVP in a losing effort, a dejected Namath walked off the field after the 21–17 loss, but the whole country had witnessed his heroics on national television. Hunt and Werblin waited by the Tide bench and handed Joe a pen. Namath removed his helmet, signed the contract on the sidelines, and changed the future of football.

—⁓—

The following day, newspaper in hand, Dorothy Unitas walked into her kitchen, where her husband, Johnny, sipped coffee. She tossed the newspaper on the table. The back-page headline read: "Namath Signs with Jets for $427,000."

"The article says that in high school, Namath's nickname was Joey U," Dorothy said. "And that the $400,000 quarterback is another Unitas."

Johnny U sipped and savored his coffee before looking up at his wife.

"Maybe." He smiled. "Only this kid Namath ... he's a lot richer."

Later that night, Art Modell ate a sandwich from a TV tray while his wife watched comedian Bob Hope's opening monologue.

"How about this football news, huh? Joe Namath just signed a $400,000 contract.... This kid will be the only player in history who plays quarterback in a business suit."

"What?" Jennifer Modell asked. "Namath signed for almost half a million dollars? Is any player worth that kind of money?"

"Of course not. God's not worth that kind of money. The kid's a playboy. He won't last. I can't wait to watch his first game. I hope they knock him on his ass."

Patricia picked up the newspaper and studied Namath's picture. A stunned Modell listened to his wife say, "He's cute, though. When do the Jets play their first game?"

CHAPTER THIRTY-ONE

Hardcore drinkers, such as Jackie Gleason and Dean Martin, often patronized Toots Shor's watering hole, and Namath seemed determined not to disgrace their legacy. Sonny Werblin's coming-out party for the new Jets quarterback turned into a five-hour drink fest. Reporters surrounded the larger-than-life figure.

"Joe, you're portrayed as a lady's man and a party animal." The reporter wore a gray hat with "PRESS" written across it's brim. "Can you sustain your playboy image and still produce?"

Namath wore a short-sleeve blue golf shirt, which emphasized his considerable forearms, and he appeared totally relaxed despite the showers of adulation.

"I don't know why you reporters think that's such a big deal. Frankly, I think it's un-American not to have a few drinks and spend a little time with a lady." His eyes brightened, his chiclet white teeth as clean as a nun's habit. "Besides I only drink in two situations … when I'm alone and when I'm in company." Namath never altered his contagious grin. "Come on, man. I'm no hypocrite. I don't hide anything. I like my women blonde and my Johnny Walker red."

He paused to swig his scotch.

"I drink for the same reason I hang out with pretty women. It makes me feel good … helps relieve the tension."

—◆◆◆—

The following day in his Fifth Avenue penthouse apartment, Namath gave directions to his interior decorator.

"Yeah, put a white llama skin rug in the living room. Gold plate the bathroom fixtures and buy me satin sheets. I want the pillowcases made from cheetah skins and Siberian snow leopards, and make sure you put a long bar in the living room with lots of stools. I plan on doing a lot of entertaining."

Namath took a belt from a beer bottle and stood in front of his penthouse view.

"Man, I want to swallow New York whole. I can't wait to hit those streets. I feel like a five-week-old puppy."

—◊◊◊—

Never one for understatement, Howard Cosell boasted that Namath's signing was the most important in the history of football. The public seemed to agree. Shea Stadium's phones rang like a bookmaker's office. Customers clamored for season tickets.

"No. I'm sorry. We have no more between the 30 yard lines. I can sell you six behind an end zone."

The second vendor turned to his workmate confidentially.

"If you have friends that need season tickets, let me know. I bought twenty on the 45 yard line. You should get your hands on some too. I'm scalping them at double face value. Everybody with a lick of sense is going to make a buck off this kid with the white shoes."

—◊◊◊—

The fervent fans packing Shea Stadium on opening day clearly felt the start of a new era. A far cry from the previous owner's pall of poverty, the atmosphere and ambiance of enthusiasm indicated that a new wave of class and optimism had descended on this AFL team.

In the owner's box, high above the mass of humanity, Lamar Hunt sipped a Coke and turned to his host, Sonny Werblin.

"I've never rooted against my own team before. It's an odd feeling. I was ambivalent this morning, but if the Jets beat Kansas

City today, it'll help make our league solvent. That's more important to both of us than any one game."

Both stood for the national anthem, and Sonny said, "Win or lose today, I'm not worried, Lamar. The Jets will catch on and so will our league. The timing is just too perfect."

As soon as the home of the brave left the opera singer's lips, Sonny sat and turned to his guest. "You're a visionary, Lamar. You're going to make your entire family proud, especially your father."

"If that's true, our league had better catch on quick. H.L's tests came back positive. My father's tumor is malignant." Lamar lowered his eyes and murmured, "I don't think he has much time left."

The final score read, Kansas City Chiefs 14, New York Jets 10. Despite that 1965 loss, Namath drew 53,658 to Shea Stadium in the Jets' first home game—more than what the New York Titans drew in all seven home games during their last season at the Polo Grounds.

His status as a star was verified. Many more Jets sellouts, both home and away, would soon follow. His brashness and charisma had captivated the public. Nothing could ever change that. Howard Cosell was right. Football would never be the same.

—∞—

Werblin's assessment of the Jets-Giants rivalry proved prescient. By the end of the '64 season, the second year the Jets had new management, the Giants had crash-dived from an 11-3 conference champion to a 2-10-2 last place team. It would be five long years before they would have another winning record.

The Jets success reaffirmed the new league's commitment to star power. They would compete against the NFL by going after the nation's very best college players. Concerned about the bottom line and conditioned to operating in the black, or close to it, the geezers of the old league were starting to feel the heat.

On a brisk May day in Namath's second season, the floors of the established league's offices looked like the stock exchange.

Team scouts and coaches screamed their draft choices while assistants checked the player's availability. Competition had taken every franchise to a new level of sophistication. Computers were now the norm, not the exception.

"This kid Otis Taylor is great, but we can't waste a pick," an NFL scout said. "How does the other league feel about him? Can we afford him? Will it get us in a bidding war? Can we hide him until he's signed?"

—⚒—

The contrast in Oakland's AFL office couldn't have been starker. Coaches and scouts stood in front of two, enormous blackboards, writing names and crossing them off. One man, more distinctive than the others, was clearly in charge. Al Davis wore slicked black hair styled in a pompadour. Dressed in chinos, pointed Italian shoes, and a striped shirt, he calmly picked his teeth.

"You want that Taylor kid? Draft him. We'll figure a way to sign him later. If we need to, we'll send him on an all-expense paid vacation to Hawaii. The other league won't even know where the hell he is. We'll pay him whatever we have to, later."

Everybody knew him as Brooklyn Al.

—⚒—

Al Davis had graduated from Brooklyn's legendary Erasmus Hall High school, whose famous alums included Barbra Streisand, Neil Diamond, and Sonny Werblin. He was smart, really smart. His IQ was 183, higher than fellow alumnus Bobby Fischer, who would become the world chess champion.

As the most popular boy in his senior class, Davis might have been its most distinctive graduate.

When he was only thirty, he was already assistant coach of the new league's Los Angeles Chargers and was extremely unpopular with his opponents. By the time Davis was thirty-three, after being named head coach of the Oakland Raiders, his arrogance and unpopularity had mutated to sheer loathing by owners of both leagues. F. Wayne Valley, the Raiders owner, later commented about hiring Davis, "We wanted someone who wanted to win so badly that he would do anything. Everywhere I went people told me what a son of a bitch Davis was, so I figured he must be doing something right."

—⚉—

AFL commissioner Joe Foss had taken his share of criticism and occasionally had battled with each of the AFL's owners. His frequent travels on behalf of the league had often made him difficult to communicate with.

In April of '66, Foss told *Sports Illustrated* about his decision to resign. "Some owners became irritated because I would never be frightened or controlled. I wouldn't call the owners and report to them every day just to gain brownie points. But I've got no regrets. Now that the league's prospering, I'm ready to move on. My mission is accomplished. It's time for me to take a rougher and bigger job."

After Foss had given his notice, the AFL owners convened in Houston and decided that for their new commissioner they needed a warrior, not a diplomat. Finding that warrior would be the challenge.

Lamar would once again rise to the challenge by appointing the thirty-six-year-old Al Davis as his new league's commissioner. Loathing would soon collect a partner, fear. The NFL owners would find out soon enough that when it came to winning, Davis was a street fighter with no scruples who would never compromise. Lamar would appoint the right man.

CHAPTER THIRTY-TWO

L amar turned on the news that evening and listened to a distraught LBJ. The weathered president announced on national television that in hopes of inducing the Vietcong to the peace table, the US would begin the carpet-bombing of North Vietnam.

The escalation did not sit well with our collective conscience. Television brought the war's irrational destruction and carnage directly into our living rooms. Endless newsreels showing our young troops frantically funneling fear and confusion into their walkie-talkies while shuttling dismembered comrades into awaiting choppers had brutalized the electorate and finally taken its toll.

For the first time, an American war was televised. Confused citizens watched footage of young healthy Marines manhandling Vietnamese grandmothers and doubted our government's strategy. This was the enemy? The madness of the war drove some Americans mad along with it.

An eighty-two-year-old peace activist watching TV in Michigan calmly exited her house and sat on her front lawn in the lotus position. Imitating protesting Vietnamese Buddhist monks, Alice Herz doused herself with gasoline and struck a match.

A father and son drove by the horror and tried to smother her with a blanket, but it was too late.

Peace advocates came in all forms. Martin Luther King joined 25,000 antiwar activists on their march through Alabama in 1965. The Southern troopers tasked with protecting the protesters seethed their contempt but said nothing. Mobs in the background hurled epithets, yet the protesters continued to march peacefully but defiantly.

LBJ and Kennedy's Secretary of Defense continued to be at odds. Slowly dragging the heel of his right hand across his forehead before glacially dragging it below his chin in desperation, Johnson placed his face inches from McNamara's. "I pushed through that Gulf of Tonkin Resolution because you and your joint chiefs assured me firepower would win this thing. That bill was like my grandma's nightgown. It covered everything. That resolution got me into this mess, and now I can't get out. I refuse to be the first president to lose a war. The North Vietnamese fired on the USS *Maddox*? For all I know they could have been shooting at seals out there. Now, thanks to you and all the other so-called 'smart fellas,' I'm knee-deep in shit.'"

LBJ looked down from the window and pointed again.

"Look at that kid's sign. 'Diem was a son of a bitch.' Like I didn't know that, goddamnit. What those kids don't understand is that we put him in charge of South Vietnam. President Diem was our son of a bitch."

The government's continuing strategy for convincing the public that the war was winnable eventually evaporated with the leak of the *Pentagon Papers* and the massive assault by the North Vietnamese at the Tet Offensive. Those two events led even the face and voice of American journalism, Walter Cronkite, to question the wisdom of our policy in Southeast Asia. When Johnson lost Cronkite, the most trusted man in America, he also lost the support of the country's majority.

On the other hand, most historians agree that even though LBJ's predecessor didn't get much legislation passed during his tenure in office, Kennedy will go down as a great president because of the consequences, intended or unintended, of his commitment to space. In the decades following his assassination, the

United States would lead the world in microelectronics, and 52 percent of all new jobs would be created by technology

—⚭—

The late president's race to the moon had men at Mission Control monitoring a manned spacecraft orbiting the earth. Many wore headphones, and to promote this remarkable achievement, the distant capsule sent live transmissions back to earth, which were then broadcasted over national TV.

The eldest of these three extraordinary men connected with Mission Control.

"That concludes tonight's transmission Houston," astronaut Frank Borman said. "We're going to grab some shut-eye, but I have one more message. You tell Tommy Nobis, damn the money. Screw the NFL. Stay in Houston, and sign with the Oilers."

The tense Mission Control staff looked at one another in disbelief and laughed. They stood, shook their heads, and gleefully flashed thumbs-up signals.

CHAPTER THIRTY-THREE

Outside of the Los Angeles Coliseum, a ubiquitous television sports broadcaster basked in his own self-importance.

"This is Howard Cosell speaking of sports. This has been an extraordinary year for professional football. College athletes are reaping the benefits of open competition for their services. Salaries have exponentially risen with the dawn of this new league. Can both leagues survive the phenomenal amounts they're having to pay for the services of kids who've never played a single down in the professional ranks? I don't think so. Something's got to give. I predict that the owners of both leagues will regret this insane escalation of player's salaries. How can they pay an untested player seven to eight times more than a ten-year proven pro? This curious sportscaster along with football fans around the nation will be analyzing the upcoming college draft with unprecedented interest."

—⁂—

In New York, the saloon's walls were lined with gauche red velvet. Empty glasses, half-filled cocktails, and stuffed ashtrays cluttered a large, rectangular table in the corner booth of the darkened bar where a trashed Joe Namath sat with a few friends. When the door whipped open, five burly, dark-suited men entered. The bar turned as silent as a crypt.

In the center of the entourage, a skinny singer in his signature straw fedora with a blue ribbon at its base stood out. The few patrons remaining stammered the singer's name in a hushed whisper, "Sinatra ... Sinatra, Sinatra." Namath's stature seemed to shrink in comparison. The entertainment giant effortlessly ate the oxygen in the room before rushing directly for the quarterback.

"Joe, I heard you were in town. I've been wanting to meet you for a long, long time. I'm glad you found Jilly's."

"Mr. Sinatra. I'm such a fan. You have no idea."

Namath jumped to his feet, but in his excitement to meet the legend, he splattered the table full of drinks all over the famous singer.

"Oh my God. I'm so sorry. Jesus, what have I done?"

As Namath blurted out a series of apologies, the hush that fell over the room reached a sepulchral tone. Well familiar with the volatile Sinatra temper, bar staffers and patrons awaited the inevitable explosion. Sinatra whipped out a white pocket square and blotted his tie and suit. The pride of Hoboken slowly straightened his lapels, reached over the table, and grabbed Namath by the shoulders.

"Ah jeez, Joe, don't worry about it. Things happen. Let's sit down and have a couple of belts."

"All my life, I've idolized you. I love your music, your style."

"Don't sell yourself short, kid. You're a star in your own right. Christ, when it comes to football, you're as big as Lombardi. You're the face of New York. Damn it. You've made this whole new league worth watching."

Joe Foss was still acting as commissioner and told a horde of reporters, "Next year two new franchises, Atlanta and Miami, will each pay $7.5 million to enter the AFL."

Watching on TV from his office, Lamar turned to the man who had once been the most critical of his Foolish Club investors, Barron Hilton.

"Seven years ago, Daddy thought I was crazy for risking $100,000. Imagine how crazy he must think Miami's Joe Robbie is?"

"Without you, this never comes to pass, Lamar." Before lifting a frosty can of Coca Cola in a mock toast, Barron beamed. "To Lamar Hunt, how the hell did I ever let you talk me into this mess?"

Lamar looked at Hilton. A salty tear clouded one eye.

"That means more to me than you can ever imagine, Barron."

CHAPTER THIRTY-FOUR

C arroll struggled with a black bow tie in front of a full-length mirror as Georgia entered their bedroom in stunning fuchsia. Pirouetting proudly in front of her husband, she blocked his reflection. Carroll scrunched his nose, marched mutely to her closet, and ripped out a black formal.

"Wear this tonight, will you, baby?"

"You're going to tell me how to dress now? You're unbelievable."

"You want to make me happy? So, make me happy."

He ignored her indignation and mused about what was really on his mind.

"I have to get the boys together. The bidding for these college kids has gotten out of hand. They're getting rich before they even touch a football. We're bankrupting ourselves. We need peace. I'm telling Rozelle that he has to work toward a merger."

"You think that's the smart move? Can't you just crush these guys? Why not just push them around? That's what you do to me."

Carroll stopped fidgeting with his tie and mockingly turned to Georgia.

"Don't give me that 'I'm just a poor rich woman and my man is a control freak' bullshit." He smirked. "You knew what I was like when you moved in."

"Yeah, I knew what you were like when I moved in."

Yet Georgia bit her tongue while he whirled back to the mirror and preached.

"Honey, a bidding war is like any other war. If we keep this up, no one wins. I hate Hunt. I hate oilmen. As a matter of fact, I hate this Southern schmuck so much that I can't even stand putting gas in my car."

Georgia unzipped her dress and walked out of it. She lifted the gown Carroll selected and carefully slid into it.

"If you think that's the smart move, you're probably right. But will the others go along?"

"The biggest gripes will come from the two teams that have to split their markets. New York's Wellington Mara and San Francisco's Lou Spadia won't be happy. The other boys will play ball. As for Cleveland, Art Modell answers to some serious people who don't like reduced profits. He'll be on board. Rozelle can't say shit. He'll do as I say, or he's gone. But as usual, it all comes down to one man, me. I've got to swallow some pride and get in touch with Hunt."

Carroll finished with his tie, turned, and admired Georgia's taut frame. The black gown hugged her the way the skin hugs a grape.

"That's my girl. See, now I'm happy."

—⁊⁊⁊—

The following day, Carroll called the office of the Dallas Cowboys.

"Hello, Clint, I might need a favor. Tex has done business with Hunt before, hasn't he?"

"Everyone who lives in Texas has done some business with the Hunts. Schramm's no different," Clint Murchison said. "Yeah, Tex knows him. He lives a few miles from Lamar in Dallas, but there's no love lost. Lamar's Texans made Schramm's job that much tougher. Look, why talk to me? I'll have Tex call you in five minutes. What do you have in mind?"

"I want Tex to reach out to Lamar with a proposition. I've got an idea but no sense explaining it twice. Maybe nothing will come of it. After I talk to Tex, I'll have him fill you in."

—⁊⁊⁊—

At dusk that same day, Joe Foss held what would be his final press conference to announce his successor. "As you already know, I'm resigning as commissioner of the American Football League. Health and personal reasons compel me to put my family first, but I'm leaving the league in extraordinary hands. My successor, a football visionary, Al Davis, wants to say a few words." He stepped back from the lectern. "Al."

Davis offered a clear contrast to his counterpart—the clean-shaven, suave, sophisticated NFL Commissioner Pete Rozelle. Davis was loud and brash. He epitomized the unmistakable touch of the Brooklyn gutter.

"As you all know, I'm the coach and general manager of the Oakland Raiders and have been in football all my life," Davis said. "But as I see it, my new job is to make the AFL the best league in pro football. The other league won't like that much, so … if my bosses need a guy who can mix it up, play a little dirty, and put constant pressure on the other league, well, I think I know a little bit about that too."

He stepped back from the lectern and asked Foss if he wanted to add anything. When Foss shook his head, Al said, "That's about it for now, fellas, but you know as well as I do that this ain't over. You'll be hearing a lot from me and a lot more from them as well. It is what it is."

What neither Foss nor Davis knew was that another get-together had taken place earlier that morning. While Al Davis was preparing to dig a collapsible tunnel under the NFL, a secretive subway was being dug under him.

The very day that Davis had accepted the commissioner's position, two men had met earlier that morning under the mammoth Texas Ranger statue at Love Field in Dallas to talk a bit of treason. As the sun rose on the tarmac, Lamar Hunt shook hands with Cowboys owner Tex Schramm. The two men strolled over to Schramm's 1966 Oldsmobile.

"Sure, we've had our differences, but you have a lot of qualities that I admire," Tex said. "You're a man of your word. You're discreet, and you have vision. Rosenbloom gave me the authority to propose a paradigm for our two leagues to merge. It's fair, and it's workable. You know as well as I that these bidding wars are madness."

Schramm was deeply tanned, his face elongated. He wore his salt-and-pepper hair military-style and brushed up stiffly on his scalp, his eyes as black as wet paint. He wore pleated gray slacks, a lavender shirt open at the neck, and oxblood loafers.

Hunt, markedly different now, was dressed elegantly as well. He was also more cynical, his language less guarded, coarser.

"I've heard all this horseshit from you boys before," Hunt said.

"The previous talks collapsed because the old guard would only accept the successful clubs from your league and not all of them," Tex said. "That's about it, right? That was the main glitch?"

"I gave all those men my word, dammit!"

"The owners will accept every team in your league now, but you have to realize that the two teams in the major coast markets, Mara and Spadia, will want compensation. Rosenbloom feels that the only sticking point to a merger will be money."

Tex Schramm knew that the merger was the right move and admired Hunt's foresight. Tex knew something about the right moves. A reporter once wrote that Schramm was so prescient that he could reminisce about the future. He added to the Dallas franchise such perceptive innovations as the first cheerleaders and the "ring of fame," where he would plaster the names of their best players on his stadium's walls. He along with Bob Ryan of NFL Films, also coined the term "America's Team," which helped make Dallas the most successful franchise in league history.

"If the amount is not unreasonable, we can do business," Hunt said. "To grow my fan base, I need AFL cities to know that we're committed and aren't going anywhere. I don't give a shit if we fly the NFL banner or not. I've given this a lot of thought. There should be two conferences, with two commissioners—"

Schramm cut Lamar off mid-sentence.

"I'm afraid that's impossible. The owners insist on one commissioner, and it must be Pete Rozelle. That part of the deal is non-negotiable."

"That could get a bit sticky. If Al Davis knows that I'm eliminating his position, it's unlikely he'll be cooperative. And if I keep Davis in the dark, I'll have to negotiate with each AFL owner separately. I dislike double-dealing, especially with Al Davis … but shoot, there's so much at stake…. Give me two weeks to think about it. We'll talk again."

CHAPTER THIRTY-FIVE

W hile shapely young women served them burgers and beers at a sports bar in Houston, Lamar and Bud Adams ignored the shorts and halters to concentrate on the business at hand.

"This is all smoke and mirrors, Lamar. Those bastards in the NFL won't negotiate in good faith. We already know what kind of men they are," Adams said. "These are the kind of outlaws that break your leg and sign your cast. They're out for themselves. They don't have the same common bond we have. We put our collective gains ahead of individual profit. When Harry recommended splitting up the television revenue equally, that alone saved four or five of our teams."

"But this merger helps everybody. Everyone on their side knows that it's smart business. A few narrow-minded traditionalists might fight us at first, but after those fools cave, they will profit as much as the visionaries. I guarantee you that they're discussing the long-term benefits of this merger right now."

Lamar was right as usual. To fine tune the particulars of the merger and the amount of compensation that they'd settle for, Mara from the Giants and Spadia from the San Francisco 49ers met with Pete Rozelle in New York over dinner.

"My family has had a team since the league's inception," Wellington Mara said. He was of medium height, broad in the shoulders, and thin in the face with chiseled, distinguished good looks. The gruff dialogue spurting from his lips seemed counterintuitive. "Those cocksuckers can't compensate me enough for my humiliation. I'd rather fight. I can't grab a newspaper without the back page taunting me with Namath's pretty boy face smiling through the faceguard of a Jets helmet."

"The Bay Area sport's market is already thin enough," Spadia's face was squat with a pug nose and a firm terse mouth. "Screw this. Why would I share my market with Oakland? Compensation? How do I put a price on somebody trying to steal my livelihood? I'm with Wellington. Let's obliterate them."

"Relax, boys," Rozelle said. "This merger will never happen. The AFL owners will never make the other NFL owners happy. You think that you're the only two owners with gripes? Their side has them as well. Oakland and the Jets don't want to share their fans either. Even if the old guard clears that hurdle, Congress would never approve. This potential merger violates the Antitrust Act. Congress won't allow a monopoly. It's only Rosenbloom that's adamant about this alliance…. I just can't figure out why. Don't worry, gentlemen. I'm still the commissioner. I won't let this merger happen."

CHAPTER THIRTY-SIX

Lamar and Norma Hunt sat in a dimly lit, mahogany-paneled octagon snug. The silverware and glass goblets sparkled invitingly on a linen-covered table displaying two place settings. Beneath their feet, the dark blue carpet was luxuriously deep, and the candles flickering atop the white tablecloth implied that the night was special.

"All right, sweetheart," Norma said. "I'm bursting with anticipation and so are you. What's the occasion? You're dying to tell me something."

"Before I tell you my news"—Lamar handed Norma a small gift-wrapped box—"A little out of character for me—you're usually not impressed with jewelry—but I had it made for you, anyway."

Norma tore off the packaging and grabbed her chest.

"Oh, Lamar, it's beautiful, absolutely gorgeous. I've never seen a bracelet quite like it."

"And you won't, either. It's unique. The two smaller rows of diamonds on the outside represent the two football leagues. The middle row has diamonds twice the size of the outer ones. Can you guess why?"

"Don't tell me?"

"Tex Schramm made contact with me. The NFL wants the merger. That means I'll finally have an NFL team."

"Oh, Lamar, I knew this would happen. I'm so proud of you ... really. I knew your chances for this merger were slim, but once you set your sights on something, it always comes to fruition. You were committed to making this happen, yet your Creator always came first and foremost. It's him that I'm really thankful to."

"I wanted to tell you in the perfect environment. This proves I was right, honey. The owners realize that everyone profits with growth. Expansion makes the league stronger. I'm glad H. L. will still be around to see this."

Norma gushed at the bracelet on her wrist.

"It's overwhelming. Where would I ever wear it?"

"Wear it? That's easy. Wear it to the first AFL-NFL championship game."

—⟋⟍—

The following week, Ralph Wilson from the Buffalo Bills and Pete Rozelle met at Miami's Sea View Inn to cement the plans for the new alliance.

"Most of the owners in our league favor the merger, Lamar especially, and he's our leader," Wilson said. "You fellows have the larger markets, so naturally we're afraid that if the bidding wars continue, some of us will go broke in the upcoming drafts. But make no mistake. Even though you're the established league, you'll take a financial beating too. Only the players will benefit."

"We are now prepared to absorb your entire league, every team," Rozelle said. "But because of the financial disparity between television contracts, we can't actually merge until 1970. Until then, we'll placate the fans by playing two interleague championship games. That'll whet their appetite for two years, and then we'll complete the union of the two leagues."

Wilson extended his hand. Rozelle, a man so duplicitous that he barely threw a shadow, turned the corners of his mouth upwards and shook Wilson's hand.

"So, we'll go ahead with this…. But just one more thing…. It'll cost you fellows $50 million to join us."

Wilson jumped out of his seat.

"Fifty million? Are you out of your mind? We won't pay that. The rest of our owners won't go for that. Why did you bring me down here to talk nonsense? Thank God Lamar's not here. I can't believe what I'm hearing. We thought that your organization was serious. I see now that you don't really want this to happen. It was all a con job. This doesn't bode well for any of us."

Wilson tossed his napkin on the table and stormed out. The argument had made the heat rise in Rozelle's neck, but he spread his hands the way a blackjack dealer does when changing shifts. The corner of his mouth quickly quirked up in the early stages of a sardonic smile.

—⁓—

Norma and Lamar lolled in their king bed that night discussing the disappointing telephone call from Ralph Wilson.

"It was smoke and mirrors, the whole thing an illusion. The $50 million was just a red herring. They don't want to merge. They still think we're a Mickey Mouse league, that we can't play with them. We'll never survive this, unless—"

The sports-savvy Norma interrupted. "You think that Rosenbloom told Rozelle to ask for that ridiculous amount of money to deliberately keep you out? There are still rumors about gambling in that '58 championship game. Weren't Tim Mara and Art Rooney bookmakers before buying teams? Maybe you're too honest for them?"

"Nobody could fix a championship game, honey. It's too far-fetched. After that sudden death game, the NFL conducted an internal investigation and found no evidence that Rosenbloom had bet on the game. Sure, Rosenbloom is a gambler, but so are many of the other owners. Shoot, even Ralph Wilson owns Thoroughbreds. No way Rosenbloom would bet on or against his own team. People who spread rumors like that will swear on a stack of Bibles that fishing is fixed."

"What now?"

"Their television money buys them influence on Capitol Hill, so they think they can bully us. Well, it won't happen. I want the merger, but I won't be fleeced."

"Don't stoop to their level. Remember it's how you play the game that's important, not whether you win or lose."

"I didn't start this to lose. Vince Lombardi said it best, 'Show me a good loser and I'll show you a loser.' Not this time. I'll do what it takes. No gloves, no Marquis de Queensberry.... I'm starting to understand Rosenbloom's thinking." He murmured, "If I can just think a few moves ahead ... I think these boys will finally get to hear Mickey Mouse roar."

CHAPTER THIRTY-SEVEN

Georgia dreamily readied herself for bed. She squinted into a fluorescent makeup mirror to do a little damage control. Unhappy with the view, her thoughts echoed her mother's familiar refrain.

"When your looks fade, you're used up. To them, you're just a trophy. Get what you can out of them while you can. Look what happened to me. Don't end up a has-been."

Georgia left the bathroom to join Carroll in bed.

"So, do you still think the merger is the best thing for everyone?"

"Everyone? What do I give a shit about everyone? It's the best thing for me. I've a few aces up my sleeve that I haven't played yet. Once we get this merger settled and pushed through Congress, compensation or no compensation, I'll lay down my cards and sweep in the chips."

Georgia wore blue panties and a short white T-shirt. She slid into bed next to Carroll and snuggled up. She rubbed his knee and the inside of his thigh, up and down his leg, and then slithered the flat of her hand down his chest and stomach.

"Honey, I think—"

Carroll clasped her hand and turned his back to her. "Not tonight, Georgia, please."

When someone loves you, even the way they pronounce your name sounds different. Georgia suddenly felt her name wasn't quite as snug in Carroll's mouth as it once was.

"What the hell is wrong with you lately? I thought power was supposed to be an aphrodisiac. I remember when you couldn't keep your hands off me. Now all you talk about in bed is business. You don't have anything going on the side? Do you?"

He glanced over his right shoulder. "What are you talking about? Of course not. You have nothing to worry about. You're the only woman in my life. I'm just preoccupied with all this aggravation. Although I think I've figured a way to make it all come up roses."

"When do you plan on telling me?"

Carroll spun over and stared at the ceiling.

"When I'm ready, you'll know. First, I've got to take care of Congress, and I know exactly how to handle that crew. You, of all people, should remember the night we met. Remember whose party it was? If anyone can squash antitrust legislation, it's old Joe."

"Kennedy can push this through?"

"Who has more connections?"

"Speaking of connections, we've lived together for eight years," Georgia said. "If something happens to you, where do I stand? It's about time you made an honest woman out of me. I want a merger too. Set the date."

"With all that I've got on my mind, you spring this, now? Your timing couldn't be worse. Don't worry. If something happens to me, I've got you taken care of. You'll get the team."

"You'll have one less thing to worry about once we're married. I'll start making plans. Now let's close that deal, and I don't mean with a handshake."

Georgia bit Carroll's neck and rubbed his chest.

"I can't right now, baby. I'm just crazy busy, too much on my mind. I just can't. You understand, right, baby?"

"Sure. Fine."

Georgia rolled away in stunned disbelief. She made a sound that wasn't quite a word before reaching below the bed, grabbing her teddy bear, and hugging it. Her twisted face turned to her mother's picture on the bed stand.

—m—

She awoke first, snuggled alongside Carroll, and plunged her hand playfully below the covers.

"Let's start the morning off with a bang."

"Jesus, honey. I have a million things to do. That's the last thing I need."

Georgia bounded out of bed and stormed to the bathroom, her face springing into a furious rage.

"Set that date," she barked.

CHAPTER THIRTY-EIGHT

Lamar Hunt had to make an announcement. It wasn't life or death, but it would be anything but easy. He had to somehow break it to the volatile Al Davis that the potential merger negotiated behind his back had gone wrong.

"So, these meetings had been going on all this time, and I knew nothing?" Davis squawked. "How the hell can I be the league's commissioner if you keep me in the dark? Pay them $50 million for a merger? Untie my hands. Those old bastards won't know what hit them. By the time I'm done, the NFL will end up paying us."

"We can't afford a war, Al," Lamar said. "Peace would be better for everyone concerned."

Their argument ended when the door exploded open. An enraged Ralph Wilson bolted into the room and tossed a newspaper on Lamar's desk. He was a short man of compact wiriness with round, ruddy cheeks under short, grizzled, graying hair. His size seemed to swell inside his tan suit with the enormous range that his anger was capable of when his pride had been injured. And it had been.

"I thought we had a verbal agreement with those cocksuckers. Look at that headline. The Giants hijacked my field goal kicker. Wellington Mara had the unmitigated gall to sign Pete Gogolak. Where does he get the balls to do that to me?"

Gogolak was football's first soccer-style kicker. His unique style was increasing attendance and getting a wealth of radio and newspaper publicity for Wilson's Buffalo Bills.

"After kicking that sixty-yarder last week," Wilson said. "He's not just a kicker. He's my biggest draw."

Lamar seemed deeply troubled by this treachery, but after a few seconds of deliberation, his eyes were suddenly clear, as if a breeze had blown a dark object away. Within seconds, he broke into a grin and then an uncharacteristic fit of laughter.

"By God, I am starting to think like that conniver Rosenbloom."

He jumped to his feet in exultation.

"Calm down, Ralph. I'm well aware of how valuable Gogolak is, not only to you but to the whole league. But don't you see what this means? The NFL just handed us our merger."

Lamar turned to Davis.

"You anticipated this, right Al? You were preparing for a war? Well you've got one. What are you prepared to do?"

"Just watch."

Davis lifted the phone, the look on his seamed face riven with an avenged smile. He dialed his right-hand man, Don Klosterman.

"Hello, Don, the NFL fired the first shot this morning. Tell all your players to bring their personal phone books to their team meetings and tell them to keep quiet about it."

Klosterman was the perfect headhunter for Davis. He was a handsome, wisecracking, irreverent man with an exuberant personality that made him seem like he couldn't wait to start each day. As a scout, he made players laugh and marvel at his encyclopedic knowledge of the sport and of his familiarity with their own personal backgrounds.

Davis hung up the phone and faced Lamar.

"We'll see how many of our players have friends in the NFL. Then we'll figure out who we might be able to hijack."

"Make sure we have our scouts hit all the black colleges, Al," Wilson said. "They've got some big, fast boys down there, a lot of talent. Let's sign them too."

"Great idea, Ralph, but where we can really stick it to them is with their quarterbacks," Lamar said. "Werblin was right. They're the stars. We'll go after their big names. They wanted a war. Then by the ghost of Robert E. Lee, we'll give them one."

—ɯ—

That same afternoon, a group of shell-shocked NFL owners sat and stared at a newspaper on the conference table. The headline read, "Giants Sign Gogolak."

"Oh my God, Wellington," Modell said. "Why didn't you tell me you needed a kicker? I would have given you one. Do you realize what you've done?"

"You're one of my best friends, Well," Art Rooney said. "But you've eaten the pig's ass here, me boy. You've put us all in jeopardy."

"You guys are overreacting," Mara said. "My Giants own the headlines again, and our markets are much bigger. What the hell can that Mickey Mouse league possibly do about it?"

CHAPTER THIRTY-NINE

Besides being the league's new commissioner, Al Davis did double duty as Oakland's coach and G.M. A redheaded assistant chalked the names of potential draft picks atop available positions on a huge blackboard inside the Oakland office. Davis tapped the redhead's shoulder and gave him a lopsided grin.

"I've stolen Ditka from Chicago, Brodie from San Francisco, and Roman Gabriel from Los Angeles," Davis said. "I would have scavenged the Giants, too, but those ancient assholes are near bottom already. I'm close to signing seven of their quarterbacks. By the time I'm done, they'll hang that maggot Mara by his heels."

Another assistant interrupted. "Mr. Davis, you have a phone call."

Davis lifted the phone to his ear and listened to his quintessential closer, Don Klosterman.

"Wilson was right. These Black colleges are full of untapped talent. Wait until you see this guy that I just signed, Al. He's as big as a beer truck and can run 100 yards in less than eleven seconds with a goat under each arm. Grambling alone has several players I want to take a closer look at. Believe me. This guy, Buck Buchanan, is 6'7" tall, 285 pounds, and he's just the start."

"Don't look at these kids too close or for too long. Sign them," Davis said. "Get their names on contracts before the NFL counteroffers. Meanwhile, I'll keep hitting those pricks where it hurts the most, their stars in the major markets."

—⁂—

In less than a month, Davis's raids had the desired effect. He had signed Roman Gabriel for $400,000, robbing the L.A. Rams of their future and any hope of Western Conference domination. Beyond raiding their talent, Davis wanted to cripple the club and handicap the organization's future.

Davis knew that by scuttling the Rams, he could dilapidate three of the NFL's largest markets. The Giants had already aged and had become a punching bag. The once-proud Chicago Bears were struggling to rise from the ashes of mediocrity. Still vibrating from the news of Gabriel's signing, the NFL owners soon learned that John Brodie of the San Francisco 49ers was about to sign with the Houston Oilers.

Hating the idea of a merger more than any other owner, Lou Spadia was apoplectic when Brodie called him with the news. The third shoe dropped when the Oilers signed the Bears' Mike Ditka, the best tight end in football. Davis had carefully thought out his plan of attack. He hijacked the two quarterbacks of the West Coast franchises and crippled the Bears passing game by thieving Ditka. The Giants were already a mess, so in less than a month, both the pirating commissioner and his enthusiastic aide Klosterman had diminished four of the NFL's major markets.

The cost of signing college prospects had skyrocketed. Pete Rozelle sat in his office, listening to television news while he re-read the memo on his desk:

> You'll get behind this merger or you'll get yourself another job. We're doing this with or without you. You fuckin' understand me? You support this merger with or without compensation or you're gone. Your BOSS, Carroll Rosenbloom.

Rozelle studied the memo again in disgust. He heard an all-too-annoying voice and glanced up at the TV.

"This is Howard Cosell speaking of sports. Owner Wellington Mara made a tragic mistake when the New York football Giants signed Pete Gogolak. The G-men were in disarray, the old grandeur dissipated. They had become losers in New York and had been reduced to a second-class franchise by the interloping New York Jets, led by their star quarterback, Joe Namath. Last month, Mara did what no other NFL or AFL owner would ever dream of doing. He signed a player formarly under contract to a team from the rival league. By signing Gogolak, Mara's piracy provoked a bidding war, and the two generals of this war, Al Davis versus Pete Rozelle, is a mismatch of cataclysmic proportions. By playing to Al Davis's strength, Wellington Mara, Pete Rozelle, and the NFL have made a tragic mistake. By signing the soccer kicker, they have brought the war down to a level that Davis can't be beaten at. Today the AFL signed three of the NFL's most glamorous stars and are negotiating with five other quarterbacks. Wellington Mara fired a revolver. Al Davis answered with a machine gun."

Rozelle crumbled the memo and disgustedly threw it at the TV.

CHAPTER FORTY

B ack in Texas, a hesitant Lamar lifted the phone, started to dial, and hung up. He glanced through his ever-present notebook before repeating the motion. Holding the receiver against his ear, he bit his lower lip before hanging up yet again. Lamar finally steeled himself, regripped the phone, and dialed.

Although Georgia was tough to live with, she was tougher to live without. Carroll had acquiesced to Georgia's "set the date" mandate, and the two had gotten married a month earlier. They were enjoying lunch when Lamar's call came through.

"Carroll Rosenbloom," he answered.

"Carroll, Lamar Hunt. We need to talk."

Carroll interrupted him. "I think it's past time that—"

Lamar cut him short. "No, Carroll, let me finish. You know this merger's right for everybody. No more games. The whole country wants to know if our boys can compete with yours. A championship game between both leagues has enormous revenue potential. Your colleagues have been shortsighted. You're not. We can make this happen. Let's have our own Appomattox. How about Washington at your earliest convenience?"

Carroll held the phone, stunned, while Lamar continued his monologue. Carroll pumped his fist in obvious delight.

"Lamar, you've read my mind. Washington it is."

A still-startled Carroll hung up, walked back out to the patio, and said to Georgia, "I've just had the most fortuitous conversation. Wait until you hear this."

—⚍—

Days after that unexpected phone call, Carroll and Georgia gathered in their Baltimore living room with Pete Rozelle, Art Rooney, and Art Modell to talk about the league's future over martinis.

"If this keeps up, we'll all be ruined," Rooney said. "There's not a lick of sense to this."

Georgia said, "Carroll has been saying all along there has to be a merger—"

"Honey, please," Carroll interrupted. "We're talking business here. Fix us another round of cocktails."

Seething at Carroll's condescension, Georgia's eyes bore into him. She stood reluctantly while brushing her fingers over the fine hairs on the back of her wrist but nevertheless took the empty glass from his extended hand.

"There's so much animosity on both sides," Modell said. "A merger will be difficult."

"We don't have to swap spit with them," Rooney said. "We don't even have to like them, but we're going to have to do business with them."

"Screw this Brooklyn Al thug," Pete Rozelle said. "Why the hell are we merging? We can win this thing."

Carroll's face hardened into a wince at Rozelle.

"'We can win this thing'? Who has their hand in your pocket? Did you get my memo? With or without you, is that clear? We need this merger. Some of our owners won't make it another year. I think I have a proposal that Hunt will accept, and I expect the support of everybody in this room."

Carroll rushed to the opposite side of the colossal chamber, opened a locked desk drawer, and retrieved a notebook. He plonked it down on a round glass coffee table the size of a truck tire.

"Art's right about the animosity. We'll need a cooling-off period. No one's thinking rationally. So, we'll let them play their league games, and we'll play ours. The television contract will have to run out by the time we play regular-season games against each other. That way we can realign the leagues before we negotiate the next contracts. Anyway, we'll need that much time to reorganize, to secure publicity, to book the hotels, and to charter flights. Here's how this has to go down."

Rosenbloom read from the notebook.

"Our league has sixteen teams; thirteen will remain with us. The other three will switch to the AFL. Added to their ten, that will balance both leagues. The teams who stay with us will collectively subsidize the three teams that switch to the tune of almost $3 million each, spread over the next five years. That should more than massage the pain of anybody's sacrifice."

Rosenbloom tossed his notes on the coffee table.

"Before anyone starts bitching, consider that the teams that pay compensation will easily make their money back in increased revenue." He lowered his eyes back to the notebook. "The AFL's attendance and television revenue will increase exponentially along with ours. No more outrageous demands for compensation. This is the smart play."

"If that's the way you want it…. But what teams will switch?" Modell asked. "And what about Congress?"

"One step at a time. Let's stop the shooting first. After a cease-fire, I'll see what can be done on the Hill. After we take care of Congress, we'll work out what teams will switch leagues."

Georgia returned and filled the empty glasses from a cold carafe. Carroll looked from one face to another and slowly lifted his martini. "To a future of unrestricted and unimaginable profit."

Georgia didn't have a glass in her hand. Instead, she placed the carafe on the coffee table and sat on the white wingback chair in the corner. Still seething, a strange transformation seemed to take place in her, as if a movie projector had switched on behind her eyelids.

In the future, Georgia wouldn't allow herself to be a beggar for scraps at the table of men who made the decisions. With her pulse fluttering in her throat, her thoughts were no longer in the present. Instead, she fumed at the all boy's club and thought, *Carroll doesn't want my input because I'm a woman. Screw that bastard. One day, he'll listen. They'll all listen.*

—◆—

True to his word, a week after their phone call, Lamar met with Rosenbloom in Carroll's D.C. restaurant, which just happened to be co-owned by Joseph Kennedy.

"I've got a few hooks in the Capitol too. Even though Lyndon's a liberal, he's all Texan," Lamar said. "Daddy was a huge booster and helped finance his career, so the Hunt name should help us get a merger through."

"I don't sit in the end zones, Lamar. Men in need of political influence must deal with both sides of the aisle. The Kennedys are my friends, but so is Lyndon and many Republicans as well. Johnson even stayed at my home in Ventnor during the Democratic Convention in Atlantic City. Lyndon thought Bobby Kennedy had contacted J. Edgar Hoover and had his hotel room bugged."

No sooner was the Kennedy name mentioned than a good-looking young man, all teeth and tan, strolled over to their table and interrupted them. Carroll smiled, leaped to his feet, and introduced Hunt to Bobby Kennedy.

"Not surprised to see you two together," Kennedy said. "The town's abuzz about a rumored pro football merger."

Acting contrary to the career politician that he was, Kennedy paused, gaping at Lamar for a moment before measuring his words.

"We've never met before. I sincerely hope you're not grateful for that. I know that there has been some bad blood between our families."

After a few uncomfortable moments, Bobby backslid to fluid form and turned to Rosenbloom. He slashed through the tension with his signature grin. "By the way, Carroll, do I call this my dad's restaurant or yours?"

"Call it anyone's you like, Senator, as long as you pay your bill."

After the three men smiled, Kennedy turned his attention back to Lamar.

"Your family and mine have been adversaries, of sorts, for years. Let's put that behind us." Kennedy cautiously continued.

"I'm not just my father's son. I'm my own man. Our family's history shouldn't affect our relationship"

He offered his hand to Hunt. After Lamar shook it, Kennedy spoke softly to Carroll.

"Give me a call at my office tomorrow morning. We'll see what can be done about that antitrust legislation. Lyndon and I can handle the Democrats. It's Dirksen and the Republicans you need to convince. A few promises and a nourishing campaign contribution might convert them."

"Dirksen and I are old friends, Bobby," Carroll said. "You remember when I first met Georgia at your dad's party? Everett was with us. It's nice to know that you and the president are in our corner."

"We'll do what we can," Kennedy said. "But follow up with those Republicans."

He offered his hand.

"Good luck with your negotiations."

"Thanks, Bobby," Carroll said.

After Kennedy left, Lamar raised both eyebrows, tilted his head, and spurted, "Well, that was a tad awkward. You probably didn't know that my father generated anti-Kennedy sentiment in Dallas days before the president's unfortunate assassination. Dad loved Lyndon and thought that Joe Kennedy bought his son's election using the Mob in Chicago. Right-wing propaganda was so strong in Texas that when the president was assassinated, my brother was questioned by the FBI. The Secret Service even insisted my father leave Dallas for his own safety. I'm delighted but a bit surprised that Bobby's helping us."

Lamar poured water from a pitcher sitting on the table and gulped it.

"I sue for antitrust violation, and it's thrown out." He shook his head. "You want to skirt antitrust regulations, and all it takes is a lunch and a promise. Now, one of the Kennedys wants to help me—amazing how Washington works."

As Carroll basked in Lamar's praise, a striking young redhead with a Russian accent approached their table.

"Rosenbloom. Is that really you? It's been a long time."

She wore leather pants, a white wool sweater, and a broad smile.

"Masha, how wonderful.... How long are you in town for?" Carroll asked.

"I've been transferred to Washington temporarily," she said. "So, here we are, two poor, lonely refugees alone in a cold, strange city. Whatever shall we do?"

She had her red hair tucked up under a white beret, but one side of it had fallen down on her neck. Her lipstick was bright red, and she wore too much of it. When she parted her mouth and leered at Lamar, even he felt uneasy.

"First we'll need champagne," Carroll said. "Lots of it."

Carroll followed Masha's eyes over to Lamar.

"We're done here, right, Lamar? An old friend ... you understand...."

Carroll turned his attention back to the redhead and said, "I'm scheduled to fly back to Florida in the morning, but let me make two quick phone calls. I'll prove to you that Washington's anything but cold."

CHAPTER FORTY-ONE

The leader of the Senate knew the power of a phone call as well.

"Senator Boggs, please. Tell him Everett Dirksen." He massaged the back of his neck while waiting.

"Hello, Hale, this is Everett. Your vote for Lyndon's civil rights bill didn't sit well with your constituents in Louisiana. I've got legislation in front of me that merges the two football leagues. If it passes, it'll mean an NFL franchise for New Orleans. You should get behind this. It'll bring a lot of votes back to your side."

"That legislation would violate antitrust restrictions," the Louisiana senator said. "The Democrats will never let it pass."

"I've been assured that the right Democrats will support it, and Lyndon will sign it," Dirksen said.

"Well, then, maybe that dog will hunt," Boggs said. "If that's the case, I'd be a fool not to get behind it."

—⚏—

A month after Dirksen's phone call, Pete Rozelle made an unprecedented announcement.

"The particulars of this historic merger are on the press handouts in front of you, gentlemen. I'll summarize the highlights: one combined league and one commissioner. The two leagues will play a championship game starting in 1967. But regular-season interleague play won't start until 1970. Of course, all of this is contingent on Congress approving the alliance. Your handouts have the specifics. That's it. I will not be taking questions at this time. It's all on the handouts. Thanks for your attention."

—𝕞—

After Rozelle's statement, the phones in NFL headquarters rang nonstop. Multiple frenetic secretaries droned the same sentence.

"I'm sorry. The league won't comment about the merger at this time."

After echoing the same message over and over, Rozelle's private secretary changed her tone.

"Please hold a moment, Mr. McPhail. I'll check."

She punched an intercom button and said, "Mr. Rozelle, we're handling all calls, but I have Mr. McPhail on the phone. He sounds upset."

"Thank you, Clara. Switch Mr. McPhail to my private line."

Rozelle strode to his desk and lifted the extension.

"Hello, Bill. I'm glad you called."

"Don't 'hello, Bill' me, you double-crossing son of a bitch. Are you telling me that I signed off for CBS to fork over $2 million for the rights to telecast the NFL championship and now it's only a semifinal game? Why didn't you notify me of this?"

"It's the NFL's business, nobody else's."

"Your business? When we pay you money, that makes it our business." McPhail's lips narrowed and thinned as he paced. "You sold me a diluted product, and now you think that you can manipulate our network into rebidding for a championship game that we've already paid for? This borders on extortion. Your league is getting too big for its boots. Without television, you'd be playing to half-empty stadiums. Remember that." He slammed the phone in Rozelle's ear.

CHAPTER FORTY-TWO

P ress, television cameras, lights, and spectators packed the room. Pete Rozelle stood before the Senate subcommittee headed again by Democrat Emanuel Celler.

"This merger guarantees that pro football operations will be preserved in the twenty-three cities and the twenty-five stadiums where they're presently conducted," Rozelle said. "For local economies and consumers, this alone is a matter of considerable public interest. Without this merger, franchise failures and relocations will be imminent. Why, I believe that the survival of the league itself will be threatened."

"I understand you want to present this union in the best possible light, but I represent the American people not your business interests," Congressman Celler said. "I think that this merger is illegal, unnecessary, and that a football monopoly will eventually lead to the development of pay television."

"With all due respect to the congressman from New York, I disagree," Senator Dirksen said. "I believe that unification is not only desirable but also beneficial to the citizens of this great country. I'm not alone in my opinion. On your desk are numerous letters recommending the merger. Besides Senator Russell Long and House Majority Leader Hale Boggs from the great state of Louisiana, you'll see signatures from both sides of the aisle and even an endorsement from the president of the United States."

"I can see that I'm going to be outmuscled here, but I wouldn't sleep well without one final plea," Celler said. "It's becoming common practice for sports franchises to rip off cities in financial distress by either franchise removal or just the threat of it. Special purpose legislation submitted to Congress exclusively for football doesn't serve the broader interests of our constituents. It is my belief that the world of sports today is endlessly complex, an ever-spinning spiral of deceit, immorality, and absence of ethics."

Celler's passionate plea was heard, acknowledged, and promptly ignored, which effectively handed a small band of persuasive promoters a totally unregulated monopoly that would eventually gift them billions of dollars.

After the subcommittee's decision, an exuberant Rozelle approached Hale Boggs with an outstretched hand on the Capitol's steps.

"Congressman Boggs, this is a terrific thing you've done. I don't know how I can ever thank you enough for this."

Boggs, a veteran of Louisiana politics too long to let such transparent politeness go unremarked, turned and stared hard into Rozelle's face.

"What do you mean you don't know how to thank me? New Orleans gets an immediate NFL franchise. If that doesn't happen, you'll regret it for the rest of your putrid life, you parasite!... We understand each other?"

Rozelle's face blanched, but he managed to spit out, "Don't worry, Congressman. You'll get your franchise."

On June 6, 1966, beneath the beaming glances of Commissioner Rozelle, Senator Long, Senator Dirksen, Congressman Boggs, and representatives of both leagues, Texas's own LBJ signed the White House bill cementing the football merger.

The following year, Rosenbloom would tell hordes of press that another oil baron, John Mecom, had bought his son John Jr. fame, fun and fortune by introducing America to the New Orleans Saints. Despite Mecom Sr. having had numerous questionable business dealings with noted New Orleans Mob boss Carlos Marcello—Mecom Sr. had met Marcello several years earlier through former Louisiana Governor Huey Long—neither Rozelle nor the NFL batted an eyelash.

CHAPTER FORTY-THREE

On January 15, 1967 despite the local blackout, a crowd of 61,946 at the Los Angeles Coliseum—heavily padded with free tickets—watched the Packers play Lamar's Chiefs in the first NFL–AFL championship game. From their skybox, Bud Adams and Norma watched Lamar pace while the rest of America watched the game on both NBC and CBS.

"For the love of God, you can't go down on the field and play for them," Norma said. "Hank Schram's a great coach, and Lenny's a great quarterback. Don't worry about what you can't control."

"I just hope if we get down early, we don't lose our poise. I pray to God we keep it close. Outside of my children's births, this is the most important moment of my life."

"Pray if you want, Lamar, but you've already been blessed," Adams said. "Without you, this game never takes place. You've won already."

"We've both been blessed, Lamar," Norma said. "You arrived at this moment without compromising your integrity. That's the man I married. That's the real point, and I'll always love and admire you for it."

—m—

Keeping the game close early, Lamar's Chiefs outgained the Green Bay Packers in total yards (181 to 164) to tighten the score to 14–10 at halftime. Early in the third quarter, Green Bay safety Willie Wood intercepted a pass and returned it fifty yards to

Kansas City's 5 yard line. The turnover ignited the Packers, and they scored 21 unanswered second-half points.

The final score read Green Bay 35, Kansas City 10. Green Bay quarterback Bart Starr, who completed 16 of 23 passes for 250 yards and 2 touchdowns, with 1interception, was named MVP.

—⁓—

A crestfallen but classy Lamar wove through the crowd to congratulate the winning coach but nearly got trampled as the Packers lifted a grinning Vince Lombardi to their shoulders.

In their limousine after, Adams said to Hunt, "Well, they beat us like a tied-up goat. But like I said before, you're still the biggest winner here today."

Lamar let his modest eyes glance to the floor but soon turned to Norma.

"You might be proud of me now but wait. Just you wait. Our day will come. Mark my words."

—⁓—

The following year, the NFL's Green Bay Packers came into Miami's Orange Bowl as defending champions, posting a 9-4-1 record during the season. They went on to defeat the Dallas Cowboys 21–17 in December for the 1967 NFL championship in the infamous "Ice Bowl."

The AFL's Oakland Raiders finished their 1967 season at 13-1 and demolished the Houston Oilers in the AFL final 40–7. Despite that lopsided victory and their season dominance, most sportswriters and fans believed any NFL team was vastly superior to any club from the new league.

The two winners met in January of '68 for the second AFL-NFL championship game.

As expected, the Packers dominated the Raiders throughout most of the game. The Raiders had only managed 2 touchdown passes from quarterback Daryle Lamonica. On the other hand,

Packer's kicker Don Chandler had made 4 field goals, including 3 in the first half, while defensive back Herb Adderley returned a sixty-yard interception for a touchdown.

Green Bay quarterback Bart Starr completed 13 of 24 passes for 202 yards with 1 touchdown. Starr was named MVP for the second straight year becoming the only back-to-back winner in the game's history.

The final scoreboard read Green Bay 33, Oakland 14.

Inside the winning locker room, sportscaster Ray Scott spoke into a microphone, "The score wasn't indicative of the total domination of the Packers this afternoon. This was hardly a contest."

General pandemonium surrounded his broadcast as various members of the Packers squirted champagne at each other. Pete Rozelle handed the trophy once again to a grinning Lombardi.

The following morning at his Florida beach house, a somber Carroll Rosenbloom peered into Pete Rozelle's uneasy face.

"What was the market share?" Carroll asked grimly.

"Respectable, 51 million viewers and we got $54,000 for a thirty-second spot. Why so intense?" Pete asked.

"Because the longer the AFL remains inferior, the slower our market will grow. I learned a valuable lesson during that Giant–Colts overtime game in '58, Pete. The American people want drama. Tension creates drama, no drama, no interest."

"Well, we can only hope for a more competitive contest. We can't control the outcome."

Carroll stirred his drink and stared into space.

"No, of course not," he said. "How could we possibly control the outcome?"

CHAPTER FORTY-FOUR

Shortly after that game, freed from his football obligations, Howard Cosell interviewed the brash, loudmouthed heavyweight champion Muhammad Ali.

"Muhammad, you're telling the American public that you're a conscientious objector, that your religious convictions forbid you to enter the US military?"

Ali was big. Big in the way that many great athletes are, not crazy tall or wide, just big. He had size, intimidating size, lightning-quick size, bulk size. His hands, shoulders, neck, and arms didn't appear quite normal.

"The great prophet Muhammad forbids me to practice violence against my fellow man."

"Forgive me for asking this, but the American public has a right to know," Cosell said. "You climb into the ring and fight every day, yet you won't fight against the communist Vietcong?"

"I ain't running to Canada. I ain't draft-dodging. I ain't burning no flag. I'm staying right here. You wanna send me to jail? Fine. Go right ahead. I've been in jail for 400 years. I could be there for four or five more, but I ain't going no 10,000 miles to murder other poor people. You want me to shoot poor people? And shoot them for what? They never lynched me. They never put no dogs on me. They never raped my mother."

"What will happen to your boxing career, to your fans?"

"My career comes second to my religion. My conscience won't let me shoot poor brown people. What do I care about the communist Vietcong? I ain't got no quarrel with them Vietcong." Ali stared wide-eyed and proud into Cosell's eyes. "No Vietcong ever called me nigger...."

—⋘—

Although lacking a college education, Ali more than held his own when challenged by white students with a far better education than he had. He yelled at a tormenter from the steps of the University of Tennessee.

"My enemies are the white people. Not the Vietcong, the Chinese, or the Japanese. You're my opposer when I want freedom. You're my opposer when I want justice. You're my opposer when I want equality. The government won't even stand up for me and my religious beliefs, yet they want me to go and die in Vietnam. If I'm gonna die, I'm gonna die right here. Right now. Fighting you. The Vietcong didn't kill my brother, Malcolm, and they didn't kill President Kennedy, either. It's white people like you."

—⋘—

JFK's former Attorney General Bobby Kennedy was now the junior senator from New York. When Bobby was first appointed to his brother's cabinet, Republicans had screamed nepotism, but the president placated the uproar by insisting that no one knew more about his policies and principles than his brother.

After JFK's assassination, Bobby's political capital increased exponentially. Blessed with a movie star's looks and mane, Bobby decided to cash in on that capital and drive the perceived usurper LBJ from the White House. Both charismatic and intelligent, he was a campaign manager's dream.

Bobby was the heir apparent to his brother's throne, so his supporters were willing to overlook Bobby's early ties to Joe McCarthy and accept him as an intense New York liberal. Even now, decades later, one cannot determine where Bobby stood on such a straightforward issue—morally if not politically—as our American misadventure in Vietnam. Nevertheless; the left wing flocked to him.

After all, differing with LBJ on what cities in North Vietnam should be bombed didn't even constitute alternative policy, never mind left-wing policy. His sophisticated, liberal admirers, however, did not seem distressed by his lack of position and steadfastly refused to support the real antiwar candidate, Eugene McCarthy. Instead, they delighted in the way Bobby used the war to embarrass Johnson.

Johnson had run against Barry Goldwater and swept into office by painting the Arizona Senator as a warmonger, yet Vietnam had become long, tedious, and all-engulfing. The continuing carnival of corpses swallowed whatever good Johnson's Great Society had produced, and the electorate was simply fed up.

Lyndon Johnson knew the writing was on the wall. Still, the nation was shocked when he announced he had decided not to run for a second term.

—∞—

Even the political capital Johnson had spent on the Civil Rights Act was pushed aside and forgotten. All that the media and vast segments of our electorate could focus on was his failure to either stop or win this never-ending war. Now, only ten months after the Civil Rights Act was passed, Robert Kennedy received horrible news while campaigning in Indianapolis and had to announce to a predominately black crowd that America's leading civil rights leader had been assassinated.

"I have some very sad news for all of you. Martin Luther King was shot and killed tonight in Memphis, Tennessee."

RFK then delivered what is now considered an iconic speech, in which he said in part, "My favorite poet was Aeschylus. He wrote 'in our sleep, pain which cannot forget falls drop by drop upon the heart until, in our own despair, against our will, comes wisdom through the awful grace of God'

What we need in the United States is not division; what we need in the United States is not hatred; what we need in the United States is not violence or lawlessness; but love and wisdom, and compassion toward one another, and a feeling of justice toward those who still suffer within our country, whether they be white or they be black.

So I shall ask you tonight to return home, to say a prayer for the family of Martin Luther King, that's true, but more importantly to say a prayer for our own country, which all of us love—a prayer for understanding and that compassion of which I spoke."

RFK was greeted with applause from the distraught crowd. He is widely credited with helping Indiana remain calm on that horrible night in America.

Although the young prince incarnate was a suspect liberal at best, after his victory in California, Robert Kennedy was well on his way to winning the Democratic primary and toppling the unpopular incumbent.

Senator Eugene McCarthy had won a surprising victory over Kennedy in Oregon a week earlier and had even led young Bobby in the early California tallies, but CBS projections now gave Kennedy a comfortable lead. The networks predicted Kennedy would be the beneficiary of a record turnout by Hispanics and African Americans.

CBS was right.

Bobby had wanted to watch the California primary results with his family at a friends' home in Malibu. He changed his mind after the networks had implored him to come to the Ambassador Hotel because they had already set up cameras. As midnight neared on the West Coast, ever aware of his television image, the young prince headed to the hotel ballroom. Packed with TV cameras and cheering supporters for a victory speech, he thanked farmworker's organizer Cesar Chavez, noted the unprecedented support of Mexican Americans and African Americans, and spoke of his desire to end the Vietnam War.

"We have certain obligations and responsibilities to our fellow citizens, which we talked about during the course of this campaign—and I want to make it clear that if I'm elected president of the United States with your help, I intend to keep those promises," Kennedy said to cheers. "So, my thanks to all of you and on to Chicago and let's win there," he concluded, flashing a victory sign.

He left the microphones and started toward the hotel kitchen.

Kennedy moved slowly into the area, shaking hands, with the exuberant supporters surrounding him. Leading a platoon of reporters, photographers, campaign staffers, TV men, and with a delirious din still reverberating from the ballroom, the Senator shook hands with a kitchen worker and started to walk on.

Then the gunfire.

The shots sounded like firecrackers, pop, pop … pop, pop, pop. The chants and cheers in the ballroom turned to gasps and screams. Ironically, football's Roosevelt Grier, a member of the Rams' "fearsome foursome," tackled the shooter Sirhan Sirhan, while a voice shouted over the commotion, "Oh my God, Robert Kennedy has been shot!"

That summer all hell broke out. The city of Detroit was in flames over racial injustices. At the Democratic National convention in Chicago, antiwar students and voting Americans angry at their will being trampled rioted in the streets. Senator Hubert Humphry of Minnesota stepped into the breach of Bobby Kennedy's death and, despite the chaos outside, received the Democratic Party nomination for president. That November, Richard Nixon, once a pariah of the Republican Party, won the presidential election.

Muhammed Ali had read the signs of the times far better than anyone else had. The nation was going to hell in a handbasket. Lyndon Johnson would die four years later, a broken man, a virtual recluse, on his Texas ranch. He was only sixty-four years of age.

CHAPTER FORTY-FIVE

Sitting in the Colts training camp alongside longtime team-mate Lou Michaels, Earl Morrall turned to the sports section of the Baltimore Sun. A quote caught his eye, making his short crew cut bristle. Jets owner Sonny Werblin had been asked the difference between owning a football team and a championship racehorse.

"In football, your inventory can cause you trouble," Werblin said. "Players can have a fight with their wives or girlfriends. They can stay out late drinking. They can feud with each other. They can pop off and make controversial headlines. Racehorses go to bed early, get up early, drink water, keep their mouths shut, and do their work."

After knocking around the league thirteen years with four different teams, longtime backup quarterback Morrall was starting to feel like livestock and resented the reference. He closed the paper, stood up, and focused on the television that Michaels was watching. His resentment soon morphed to outrage.

The duo watched handsome Joe Namath, wearing a pair of white boxer shorts, shave off his Fu Manchu mustache. The song "The Stripper" blasted in the background while a beautiful blonde (Farrah Fawcett) seductively swooned at him. A smiling Namath lathered with Noxzema and ran the blade under his nose and down his chin.

"Take it off, Joe. Take it all off," the blonde crooned.

"In the league three years, and he earns $15,000 to shave his mustache!" Morrall yelled to Michaels.

"He's making more for this commercial than either of us made for the entire season when we first broke in," Michaels countered.

"No one has ever asked us to make a commercial. I'd shave my ass on TV for fifteen grand. If this kid's worth $400,000, then I'm worth a million."

Tom Matte ambled into the locker room and asked, "What the hell were you two guys watching that's got you both so riled up?"

"We were watching this kid from Alabama teach us what we should have learned a dozen years ago," said Michaels. "Forget about the glamour. That fades as fast as the next hot kid who comes along. Grab the cash while it's there."

"Remember when I was getting that long needle between my toes for that ankle problem?" Morrall chimed in. "Well, I used to picture Rosenbloom counting the gate receipts from the Stadium Club where the players aren't invited, sipping martinis next to the governor. The owners never gave a shit about us. We're just hunks of meat. They don't even care about the game. It's all about the money. Men have died playing this game, hundreds maimed by it, and countless players disgraced trying to play it, while the owners sit and watch from skyboxes sitting on their fat wallets. What suckers we are."

The salary wars notwithstanding, football had another problem in 1968. Baseball was threatening to reclaim America's sporting consciousness. Veterans like Willie Mays, Hank Aaron, Roberto Clemente, and Mickey Mantle were still active while exciting fresh players like Johnny Bench, Rod Carew, Tom Seaver, and Reggie Jackson, all of whom would become first ballot Hall of Famers, were rapidly attracting the younger generation.

Pitchers were stars too.

Don Drysdale pitched 58 2/3 scoreless innings, and Catfish Hunter became the first American League pitcher to throw a perfect game since the Yankees' Don Larson in 1956. While their city was burning, the Detroit Tigers also caught fire, sparked by Denny McClain's 31 wins, the first pitcher to accomplish that since Dizzy Dean in 1934. Bob Gibson had a microscopic 1.12

ERA for St Louis, the lowest in fifty-four years. Detroit went on to whip the Cardinals in a thrilling seven-game series, despite Gibson having struck out seventeen Tigers in a Game One win.

No doubt about it, goddammit, baseball was exciting again.

Because football's first two championship games were ho hum affairs, the AFL had to do something and fast. With Lamar's foresight, and more than a little help from the old regime, they did.

With the second AFL-NFL championship game a distant memory, Lamar watched his son drop a ball onto the hardwood floor. The ball bounced all the way to the living room ceiling.

"I've played every kind of ball you can imagine, but I've never seen one bounce that high. What kind of ball is that?"

"It's a Super-Ball, Dad. Wham-O makes them. It bounces three times higher than a regular ball. Everybody's playing with them."

Lamar picked up the ball and examined it.

"Let me see that. A Super-Ball, huh? I wonder what it's made of?"

Lamar handed the ball back to Lamar Jr. and strolled over to a large picture window while letting his mind drift.

It was bright and warm outside, and a rainbow haze drifted across the lawn from the water sprinklers. The oak trees were green and etched against the clear blue sky. Down at the mansion's entrance, by a huge, live oak whose roots had cracked the driveway, a Mexican man was trimming bushes. Lamar reviewed the landscape absentmindedly for a minute or so, and then looked back over his left shoulder at his son and said, "A Super-Ball?"

With his manic mind still echoing his son's conversation, Lamar dialed Pete Rozelle.

"Hello, Commissioner, I'm not bothering you, am I? Good. I was thinking about this final game."

"What game is that, Lamar, the NFL championship, or the AFL championship?" Pete asked.

"No, no Pete. The last game, the final one, the final championship game, what do you call it? When the two leagues meet, you know, the Super Bowl?"

"The Super Bowl...? Oh, you mean the NFL–AFL championship game. What about it?"

"This might be a frivolous idea, but I thought you might add some class to the presentation."

"What do you mean? How?"

"Let's call it the Super Bowl and put Roman numerals after it. That would add a little zing. I always thought the packaging of that final game was a little lackluster. It's a small thing and yet...."

"Let us worry about the packaging, okay, Lamar? By the way, how's your dad doing?"

"Bad news, Pete. He's terminal."

—〰—

Although the NFL was determined to control every aspect of their marketing, some things were beyond even Rozelle's control. The press got wind of Lamar's idea and decided that the phrase "the AFL-NFL championship game" took up too much space. In journalism's never-ending pursuit to save time and ink through brevity, the Super Bowl suited them just fine.

The public likes to think that the things that made the Super Bowl the ultimate holiday are the results of happy accidents. On the contrary, seat-of-the-pants decisions made decades ago have since proved prescient. The addition of Roman numerals quickly became the norm, and those two marketing maneuvers were among many that took a normal football contest and elevated its status to what caused Norman Vincent Peale to remark, "If Jesus were alive today, he'd be at the Super Bowl."

CHAPTER FORTY-SIX

B y the fall of '68, old-guard Republicans and their younger pacifistic counterparts divided the sentiments of the country. The three networks transmitting a seemingly endless array of corpses returning home for burial only helped enflame the constant chaos in the streets. Americans were exhausted from the Vietnam War and needed something to distract them from the mayhem. They needed the circus of football to deliver them from the realities of life.

In November, an American Football League game delivered the diversion they craved. The Jets played Oakland, and each team brought a 7-2 record and hopes of a postseason run to this nationally televised game—a broadcast that would go terribly wrong and confirm that the words bad and publicity have no place in the same sentence.

The game was fraught with tension. First Namath's Jets scored then Daryle Lamonica's Raiders countered. Oakland would take the lead. New York would tie it. Back and forth throughout the game, like a tennis match. With the Jets clinging to a thin 32–29 lead, less than a minute remained. Oakland had the ball on the Jets 40 yard line. A tall, thin man wearing a bronze overcoat and a brown fedora entered the sound booth and murmured into the sportscaster's ear. Curt Gowdy's hand shielded the microphone.

Gowdy nodded his head and spoke into his mic. "Unfortunately for our affiliate stations, my producer tells me that we have to switch to regularly scheduled programming. So, for those of you who won't see the close of the game, stay tuned for NBC's special production of Heidi."

Millions of viewers were force-fed Heidi while the Raiders' Daryle Lamonica tossed a long touchdown bomb to rookie Charlie Smith. The Jets fumbled the ensuing kickoff, leading to another score. The Raiders scored 14 points in fewer than nine seconds, and dumbfounded football fans were robbed of the remarkable fireworks.

—〰—

That same day inside NBC studios, the AFL's newfound popularity was demonstrated by the thousands of complaints that lit up their switchboard, the "Heidi Bowl's" cataclysmic aftermath. The volume blew up the NBC switchboards. Fans threatened to call police stations and annihilate their exchanges too. One irate caller screamed through the phone, "I hope your NBC peacock dies of feather rot!"

—〰—

"Two scores in less than ten seconds," the fired NBC executive moaned. "That's not football. That's basketball. The fans complain, switchboards light up, and I'm history. Oakland 43, Jets 32, unbelievable. With my luck, if I bought a cemetery, people would stop dying."

—〰—

Six weeks later the two teams met again in the AFL championship game. The winner would advance to the newly christened Super Bowl. On game day that cold December morning, John Timoney, a hard-nosed rookie cop who would go on to become the youngest chief of department in New York City history, left his station after his Saturday night shift. He spotted Joe Namath leaving a Midtown hotel wearing his signature $5,000 white mink coat. A bottle of Johnny Walker Red filled one of Namath's hands and a blonde the other. Broadway Joe stumbled onto the sidewalk like a forlorn character out of an early Irish novel.

With kickoff less than five hours away, the rookie Irish cop raced to a payphone. "Hey, Patty, it's me, John. Listen. I just left the precinct after my shift this morning and spotted Joe Namath across the street coming out of the side entrance of the Summit Hotel. He's either gooned-up or hungover. No way he'll play worth a shit today. He was with some knockout blonde in go-go boots," John said. "Bet everything you can for me on the Raiders. They're going to destroy the Jets today. Yeah, send it in. Bet the rent money. It's a lock."

Satisfied his bet was in, Timoney drove up to the Bronx to have a full Irish breakfast. He'd need fortification. He planned on spending the afternoon in his neighborhood pub, tipping a few and watching Namath piss away the AFL championship game.

Hours later that same day, Al Davis pulled Lamar Hunt aside in the owner's box at Shea Stadium.

"Lamar, step outside with me. We need to talk."

A surprised Hunt nodded, and the two strolled over to the public bar in the mezzanine outside the skyboxes. Lamar ordered a Jack Black and Coke while Davis had his Coke straight over ice.

"Lamar, regardless of who wins this game today, you have to talk with Rosenbloom." Davis's black velour warmup suit and black leather jacket stood in stark contrast to Hunt's tan wool overcoat.

"In regard to what? I'm in contact with Rosenbloom all the time. We're all partners now."

"For the benefit of the league and everyone involved, we can't have another blowout in this year's Super Bowl," Davis said.

"I couldn't agree more, Al, but we can't do anything except pray that either your Raiders or the Jets play the game of their lives."

Lamar sipped his drink as Davis leaned closer to his ear.

"We might not be able to do anything, but Rosenbloom could," Davis said.

"What are you getting at?"

"Rosenbloom can make sure the game is at least close," Davis said. "Why would he do that?"

"Because it benefits him as well as us," Davis said. "It'll guarantee parity and will exponentially increase interest and profits in future Super Bowls."

"I think I'd have a heck of a time convincing Rosenbloom that it would be in his best interest to throw the game," Lamar smiled, attempting to laugh off Davis's proposition, but his stomach was starting to spit a sickening bile.

The blood drained from Davis's face. His skin drew taut against the bone, and there was a flat, green venomous glare in his eyes. The kind of look you only see in people who had successfully worked for years to hide the capability for cunning that lived inside them. He leaned in close, and his eyes locked on Lamar's.

"Maybe. Maybe not. Think about it. Rosenbloom's a businessman. His partners in the NFL just forked over $3 million smackers to Modell and Rooney and him to switch into the so-called weaker league. If the AFL wins or even just keeps the game competitive, Rosenbloom just pocketed three million to switch into the stronger league."

"That's true enough, Al, but Rosenbloom's a fierce competitor. He'd never go for it."

"Listen, Lamar. I'd go to Rosenbloom myself and convince him it's in his best interest if I could, but the son of a bitch will never agree to a meeting with me. Everyone on their side hates my guts. I'm telling you; this won't be as tough a sell as you think. Rosenbloom's a businessman. Business is about profit, not championships. He'll not only go for a fix; he might have already thought about it himself."

"But even if he wanted to, how the hell could he pull it off?"

"Oh Christ … are you kidding? There are multiple ways to do it."

Lamar glanced up from his drink, suddenly intrigued.

"Harry Wismer once told me that there is an infraction on every single play in the NFL."

Lamar took a swig of his bourbon and savored it.

"Sure, he could get to an official," Davis said.

Davis saw he had Lamar interested and was sure he would go along with the fix. It made too much sense not to.

"A coach could accidentally receive their opponent's playbook," Lamar said. "Or you could get to a key player on the offense. Multiple ways."

"Exactly," Davis said. "Now you're starting to get it."

Lamar spoke soft and slow.

"Look, this game brings to fruition everything I've prayed for. If our league keeps the Super Bowl close or even wins, no one will be happier than me. I just can't bring myself to go to Rosenbloom and ask for something so totally alien to everything I believe in. What if he says no? Worse yet, what if he says yes? The Bible says, 'what does it profit a man if he gains the whole world but suffers the loss of his soul?' I wouldn't sell my immortal soul to gain the entire world, yet you're asking me to compromise everything I believe in for a sporting event?"

"Lamar, you once sold me out by negotiating behind my back with Clint Murchison for the common good, the good of the league. Did I hold a grudge? Hell, no. I knew you made that misguided decision for the overall good. Don't you see? This is the best thing that could happen to all of us. The best thing that could happen to our league."

"Oh, I get it, Al. I might not be from Brooklyn, but I understand the concept of cheating to attain a short-term—"

Davis interrupted him.

"Let's talk hypothetically. Suppose the other owners gave me $3 million to shift to the weaker league, but after I switched, the weaker league turned out to be the stronger one. It would make the other owners look like fools. Let's further suppose because, after all, we're just supposing, that I was a gambling man. I could make a sizable bet on the Jets plus more than 2 touchdowns and make a killing."

"That's a lot of supposing. Let's look at it from another viewpoint. What if our Raiders or Jets were to beat their NFL team legitimately? Your plan robs us of the satisfaction of beating them fair and square like a football game is meant to be. No. I'm sorry, Al. I just won't do it. No way will I humiliate myself in front of

Rosenbloom by asking him to lay down against us. He still thinks we're a Mickey Mouse league. I want to beat the superiority off his smug face by following the rules. I'm surprised you would even come to me with this harebrained scheme. You're lucky I don't report this conversation to the commissioner. Of course, I won't but ethically I should. Look, no hard feelings, but I think this conversation is over. You said your piece, and I listened. Good luck out there today. Watch their running game. It's more dangerous than people give them credit for." Lamar slugged his drink, covered the empty glass with a cocktail napkin, and headed back inside the skybox.

Not restrained by Lamar's religious reservations nor having an iota of Hunt's scruples, Al Davis picked his teeth and thought, *Funny how Rosenbloom was able to persuade two of the NFLs proudest and most powerful organizations, Pittsburgh and Cleveland, to switch leagues along with his Colts. Maybe, just maybe, Rosenbloom might accept a call from me after all.*

The day after the Jets beat the Raiders 27–23 in that memorable showdown, patrolman Tommy Ryan, John Timoney's partner, climbed into their patrol car. He took the folded Daily News from under his arm and turned it to the back page. Ryan said with a wry grin, "Were you crazy? Betting that kind of money on a football game?"

John turned the black-and-white's ignition key, heard the engine roar to life, and—before shifting it into drive—faced his partner disgustedly.

"Can you believe that guy, Tommy? I see him toasted five hours before game time. The Raiders pound the shit out of him, and he still plays the game of his life, 266 yards and 3 touchdowns. What are ya gonna do? That bloody Namath."

CHAPTER FORTY-SEVEN

Handsome, hairy-chested Joe Namath lounged poolside on a blue canvas deck chair wearing rust-colored swim trunks and a dazzling smile. Less than a week before Super Bowl III, reporters surrounded him, and bikini-clad girls strolled by, vying for his attention.

"Vegas has the Jets an eighteen-point underdog," the reporter said.

"Our team talked about that," Namath said. "We decided we're still gonna show up."

"Hey, Joe," another reporter yelled. "When you were at the University of Alabama, I heard you weren't much of a student. Did you major in basket weaving?"

"Nah, shoot, man, basket weaving was too tough." Namath flashed his chiclet grin. "I majored in journalism."

A young blonde in a pink bathing suit, terry-cloth robe, and high heels walked by and pouted at Namath.

"Poor Joe, reporters just won't leave you alone. What you need is someone to take your mind off the big game."

Joe grinned, winked, and then turned his attention back to the reporters.

"The oddsmakers are wrong. Earl Morrall is their league's MVP? Shoot, we have five or six quarterbacks in our league better than Morrall, including me." He grinned wider. "If Morrall played on the Jets, he'd be third-string."

"The Colts linebackers say that this is a mismatch!" another reporter shouted. "Your interception-to-touchdown ratio stinks. Your defense is suspect, and your knees are shaky."

"I've got two things more important than knees or ratios— guts and a great offensive line."

Reporters crowded the Colts workouts, hungry for a pre-Super Bowl story or controversy. Semi-nude men sporting crew cuts populated the locker room. While a few slowpokes leisurely removed white shirts and ties, a reporter approached Shula.

"Namath said that if Morrall played on the Jets, he'd be third-string and rated him behind his backup quarterback Babe Parilli. How do you feel about that, Coach?"

"Where does Namath get off knocking Earl?" Shula said. "He took over for an injured Unitas, had an MVP season, and Joe mouths off about him? Earl's an old pro. He won't make mistakes. Namath thinks he's bigger than the game. We don't need his quotes to fire us up. Our team knows what's at stake. We'll do our talking on the field."

In stark contrast to the Colts, a radio flooded the Jets locker room with Steppenwolf's "Born to Be Wild." Long-haired men weaved blow-dryers in front of a dozen bathroom mirrors. One player zipped up Beatle boots while rifling the floor of his locker for the small chocolate pelt saddlebag that he wore over his left shoulder. Coach Weeb Ewbank stood on a bench and demanded the team's attention.

"Good practice today, men. You've seen the game films, so whatever they throw at us won't be anything new. A few teams we've played during the season have similar techniques. What I'm about to say now is important, so listen up. Tiger, turn off that music."

He waited for complete silence.

"Whatever the hell you do, after we win—and we will win—don't pick me up on your shoulders and carry me off the field." He opened his mouth as wide as a hippo. "I just had a hip operation, and you might ruin my other hip. So, I'll walk. OK?"

Ewbank's speech brought the expected results. A roar erupted. A grinning Namath lifted his right index finger in the air and pointed to the ceiling.

—w—

Later that evening, at the Miami Touchdown Club, Namath wore a white dinner jacket and black bow tie while speaking in front of the sold-out banquet. He was only minutes in when the crowd's attention shifted. A heckler sitting four rows in from the exit screamed, "You'll be playing your first pro football game Sunday, pretty boy. This is a real league. You won't be modeling pantyhose after the Colts linebackers get done with you. Your team is overmatched!"

The outraged crowd turned to shout down the heckler, but Namath was unruffled.

"Overmatched?" The smile smothered his face like a flood of light. "Listen. We're not the slightest bit overmatched. In fact, we're going to win Sunday. I guarantee it."

Out-of-town newspapers were stacked neatly on the corner of the Tropicana Hotel's check-in desk. The *New York Daily News* headline read, "Namath Guarantees It." The *Miami Herald* headline read, "Colts 18-point Favorites to Steamroll Jets." The *Los Angeles Times* headline read, "Joe Says No."

In Vegas, men formed long lines, studying football forms and cheat sheets at the Tropicana's sportsbook. A Catholic priest peeked to the front of the queue, wondering why the delay. Nobody wanted to get "shut out."

Everybody wanted to take a sip of that unquenchable high that sick gamblers call juice. When you are at the wheel of your car and hear a cop's siren behind you, the flutter in your heart and the sinking feeling in your stomach as you glance into your rearview mirror, that's juice.

And if you were lucky enough that the state trooper roared past your car, you got something for nothing. You beat the system. You covered. That's the rush. Life is a gamble. Everybody gambles, every day, everywhere. Like H.L. Hunt said, if Lamar's league was to succeed, it would be because of gambling, not in spite of it.

The action wasn't confined to American shores. Over the din of the bells, whistles, and clanging metal plates of slot machines, crapshooters in Monte Carlo's casinos screamed "seven come eleven" in three different languages. Every roll promised momentary prosperity. Long lines of designer-clad men and women overwhelmed the betting windows looking for juice on American football. The whole world wanted action on this game.

Far from the legitimate casinos and elite Mediterranean crowds, three Bronx men hoped for a Jets victory. No, not hoping for it. On that particular Lord's Day, these three bookies were praying for it, and they prayed hard. Not the way the faithful pray in churches but the way only desperate gamblers pray.

—⁊⁊⁊—

An anxious middle-aged bookie vaulted the stairs of a graffiti-scrawled South Bronx walk-up. He scaled flight-by-flight, passing two piles of dogshit and a used syringe before stopping at an apartment door. Marshall tumbled the lock and walked into a sparsely furnished living room. He threw his brown leather jacket on a lopsided sofa. It missed its mark and crumbled to the floor next to the sofa's broken leg.

Ignoring both, he hustled into a converted bedroom where a large, white dry erase board read "Colts 17 1/2. Over and Under—40." On the table beneath the odds rested four rollover phones and a collection of pens and betting slips. Red and Blinky wore dark slacks and sweaters. Both lifted phones, barked numbers, and furiously scribbled on betting slips. Blinky's glasses covered squinty eyes, and he jumped up irregularly to change numbers on that all-important dry white erase board.

Marshall grabbed the only free phone and began scrawling.

"Wait a minute. Wait a minute. Shut up a second. Don't hang up," Marshall said. "Wait for your repeat. Tommy for Red, you got the Colts minus 17 1/2 for two G's."

Blinky barked through the phone next to him.

"Yeah, Joe C for Red," Blinky said. "We are using Colts minus 17 1/2 for a thousand. Wait. Let me read it back. Don't hang up ya Greek prick. Let me read it back. Joe C, you've got the Colts minus 17 1/2 for a grand."

"Jesus Christ that's $21,000 more we have on the Colts," Blinky said. "Red, maybe you should call that big office in Brooklyn and get a fresh line?"

"Good idea," Marshall said.

The two continued to scribble.

"Brooklyn just went to 17," Red said.

Marshall's jaw dropped.

"What, 17? How could they go to 17? We haven't written a Jet ticket yet, and we're in New York. It's gotta be the same all over the country. Who the hell is betting all this big money on the Jets? Why in the hell did the line go down? I don't get it. But those Brooklyn guineas are sharp. We gotta pay attention. Get updates every five minutes."

Marshall shook his head and began a self-serving rant.

"The more I take action, the more I'm convinced this shit ain't on the level. Think about it. Gambling around the world is dominated by organized crime, and even from our viewpoint, sports must appear to be clean. If the public thought for even a minute that a game was fixed, our phones wouldn't be ringing off the hook. I heard on the radio yesterday that when Rozelle was asked about why he conferred with notorious bookie, Lou Chesler, on point spread fluctuations, he had the balls to say, 'We have common interests.' Can you imagine? Holy shit. He's a bookie for Chrissakes. Common interests, my ass.'"

"We're going to take some beating today," Red said. "The Colts are going to blow this team out. They destroyed the Browns to get here. They've lost, what, one game in two years? They've got the player of the year with Morrall; the best quarterback ever with Unitas; great linebackers with Curtiss, Lee, and Hendrix. I feel like betting the cocksuckers myself. What are you going to do? The chumps have to be right sometimes. Fuck it. We'll go to 18. Maybe it'll slow the chalk betters down a bit. Some guys might bet the Jets just to play the number."

"I'm with you, Red," Blinky said. "The first two Super Bowls were bad. This will be like Notre Dame playing St. Mary's Home for the Blind. After this game, they'll have to pay people to go see this shit."

CHAPTER FORTY-EIGHT

The next day, shielded from the sun by a brown fedora and scarf, Curt Gowdy grasped the microphone through the sleeve of a Barleycorn tweed sport coat.

"Curt Gowdy with Al DeRogatis and Kyle Rote here at the Super Bowl in Miami, where the upstart New York Jets are set to battle the heavily favored Baltimore Colts. The NFL and AFL champions have met twice before, and each time the NFL has come away as the superior league by a wide margin. The Colts are under the direction of the Cinderella Man, Earl Morrall, who took over for an injured Johnny Unitas at the start of the season. Morrall has had a spectacular campaign leading the Colts to a 15-1 record and was voted the NFL Most Valuable Player for his efforts. The 11-3 Jets, on the other hand, are built around the arm of their brash young quarterback, Broadway Joe Namath, who has guaranteed a Jets victory today. This game ought to be a doozy."

Georgia sat with an anxious Carroll Rosenbloom in the press box, along with a cadre of league dignitaries, including the Hunts, Rooneys, Rozelles, Maras, Wilsons and Modells.

"The Jets kicked off, and the Colts immediately took the ball and advanced it to the Jets 19 yard line," Gowdy recapped. "Morrall threw a perfect pass to flanker Willie Richardson, who couldn't hold on and dropped the ball at the goal line. Two downs later, the Colts called on Lou Michaels, who missed a twenty-seven-yard field goal."

Inside the press box, Lamar rotated his neck and shot Rosenbloom an antsy look.

"That brings us up to date with only fifty seconds remaining in the first quarter," Gowdy said. "Jets ball. Namath is back to pass.

He completes it to George Sauer for three yards. Sauer FUMBLES. The Colts recover at the Jets 12 yard line. Ron Porter hit Sauer and jolted the ball loose. What did you think about that, Al?"

"That could be a turning point in this game," DeRogatis said. "Whoever scores first will have a big advantage, Curt. This game is shaping up to be a defensive battle. The Colts already had one chance to take the lead. Now they have a golden opportunity deep in Jet territory."

A confident Rozelle lit another cigarette.

"It's now third and goal from the Jets six," Curt said. "Morrall throws a beauty to Tom Mitchell in the endzone. The ball is deflected off his hands and intercepted by Randy Beverly. The Jets will take over on the twenty." He turned to the third man in the booth, "Wow, Kyle."

"Morrall threw a perfect spiral but hit Mitchell in a bad place," Kyle said. "The hands." He grinned at his two boothmates and said, "The Colts should be up by 10 points by now, but we remain scoreless."

The first score finally came with 9:34 left in the first half. Broadway Joe handed off to Matt Snell, who bulled his way in from the 6 yard line. Jim Turner converted and the Jets led 7–0.

Seven minutes later, with 2 minutes, 34 seconds left in the second quarter, Morrall threw a pass intended for Willie Richardson from the Colt's 15 yard line. He was intercepted again by Johnny Sample on the Jets 2 yard line.

"Unbelievable," Rozelle said.

Unfazed, Rosenbloom poured himself and Georgia another drink.

"Well, here we are right before the half, and the Jets have stunned the crowd with a 7–0 lead over the heavily favored

Colts." Curt turned to DeRogatis. "Well, so far, Al, the game has been a series of Colt miscues. When Sauer fumbled on the Jets 12 yard line, the Colts had a chance to capitalize. But only three plays later, Earl Morrall was intercepted."

"You're dead right, Curt," Al said. "Then in the second quarter, Tom Matte's fifty-eight-yard Super Bowl record run was wasted by another Morrall interception. Despite Morrall's second miscue, the Colts defense rose to the occasion and held the Jets to three and out. Now, with a little over a minute remaining in the half, the Colts are threatening once again. They have a first and ten at the Jets 41 yard line."

"The Colts break the huddle, and Morrall lines up under center," Curt said. "He takes the snap and hands off to Matte on a sweep right. Wait a minute. It's not a sweep. Matte stops and pitches back to Morrall. It's a flea-flicker. Morrall has a wide-open Jimmy Orr in the end zone. Morrall doesn't see Orr. He throws the ball down the middle to running back Jerry Hill…. It's intercepted again, this time by Jets safety Jim Hudson."

"Unbelievable," Kyle interjected. "The Colts have shot themselves in the foot again. Incredible. That's the third interception for Morrall this half. How could Morrall not see Orr open? He did everything but shoot off a flare out there."

The contrast between the unruffled announcers' booth and the Colts sidelines couldn't have been more pronounced. Head coach Don Shula was scrambling up the Colts sidelines and screaming at every one of his assistant coaches in disbelief.

"What the hell's Morrall doing out there? How could he miss Orr? That play is designed for Jimmy. That's the same play we used two weeks ago against Cleveland. We are playing like horse-shit, just horseshit. Three fucking interceptions, what the hell is going on?"

When the first half expired, the scoreboard read, Jets 7, Colts 0.

—ɱ—

Gowdy put in words what the entire stadium was thinking. "We certainly have some surprised spectators here today, Al, including me. No one believed this Jet team had the slightest chance against a mighty Colts team that had lost only twice in their last thirty games. Joe Namath has called nearly every play at the line of scrimmage. Namath's reading the Colts defense like he knows their playbook."

In the tunnel to the dressing room, Shula accosted Morrall.

"Earl, what's going on? Jimmy was wide open in the end zone."

"I didn't see him, Don. I just didn't see him."

"Didn't see him? What did he have to do, start a bonfire?"

"I really didn't see him, Don. The halftime band was huddled near the end zone. Jimmy must have blended in with their blue uniforms."

Shula gave him an incredulous gaze, shook his head in disbelief, and then started a slow jog toward the locker room.

—ɱ—

Watching the Florida A&M marching band in a tribute to America at halftime, the AFL fans were grinning, but the NFL followers remained confident.

Carroll lifted a pack of Marlboros from his shirt pocket.

"Let me have one of those cigarettes," asked Ralph Wilson.

"You don't smoke."

"I do today."

He shook a cigarette out of his pack, set fire to Wilson's, and smiled.

"Welcome to the NFL, rookie."

Lamar watched Carroll cautiously. Usually at these games, Carroll was sweating through his shirt. Why wasn't he foaming at the mouth like Modell at the halftime score? Carroll was calm, too calm if you asked Lamar.

—⟋⟍⟋—

On the first play of the second half, the sure-handed Matte uncharacteristically fumbled, and the Jets recovered on the Colts 25 yard line. Nine plays later Turner kicked a field goal to put the Jets up 10–0. Two more field goals would follow, the second aided by a curious pass interference call against the Colts defense.

Now that the score was Jets 16, Colts 0. Rooney and Modell stirred anxiously. One half may have been a fluke. But two? Something wasn't on the level.

—⟋⟍⟋—

"With four minutes left to go in the third quarter, the Jets are pitching a shutout leading 16–0," Curt said. "After a pitiful performance by his MVP, only 6 of 17 for 71 yards with 3 interceptions, Shula finally lifted Morrall with 3:30 to go in the third. Unless old Johnny Unitas can pull off one of his patented miracles, we're watching football history here today."

The camera panned to a dejected Morrall sitting on a crowded Colts bench. Helmet off, staring into the dirt, his fallen face spoke volumes. In contrast, the entire Jets bench was empty, standing on the sidelines and staring out at the field. With Unitas in the game, invincibility had dissipated. Joe Namath watched, with an apprehensive gaze, as his childhood hero leaped into action.

—⟋⟍⟋—

"With a little over three minutes left in the game, Unitas puts the Colts on the board," Gowdy said. "The score now stands 16–7. Colt fans still hope old number 19 can save the day."

The Colts recovered the onside kick and Unitas completed three straight passes. But now, three incomplete passes later, the Colts found themselves on the Jets 19 yard line with a fourth and ten.

"Here we go folks for all the marbles," Gowdy said. "Unitas over center, he's back to pass. Unitas tries to fit the ball into tight coverage between two defenders. The ball's knocked down. The Colts have turned it over on downs. The Jets are gonna win it."

"I don't know what Shula was thinking, Curt," said DeRogatis. "The Colts needed two scores. Why not take the field goal, and go for another onside kick? This game defied all logic."

With the 16–7 score final, a triumphant Namath jogged off the field, his head down and his index finger raised skyward above his helmet. A delighted grin radiated through his facemask.

—m—

Far from the chaos of the upset, a smile crept across an old man's face. Hooked up to life-supporting tubes, a frail H.L. Hunt wearily pointed his index finger toward the hospital ward's ceiling, mimicking Namath.

—m—

After the game ended, the 75,000 fans in the stands and reporters in the press box were still stunned. They looked to each other searching for answers. One man had the answer, and he wasn't talking. He was too busy feigning disappointment. His name was Carroll Rosenbloom.

Lamar whispered to Carroll, "I've just fulfilled my wildest dreams, so why do I feel about as low as a crippled cricket's ass? I pray this has all been worth it."

"Oh, it's worth it. Savor this victory, Lamar, but don't expect accolades. The owners and fans only care temporarily. Remember what happened to Sonny Werblin?" Carroll asked mockingly. "Last year, his own partners made him sell all his shares of the franchise. Fickle fans will cheer today when Ewbank hoists that championship trophy and maybe cheer again when they're carrying his dead body out of Shea Stadium. There's no guarantee about number two. Screw the praises. Money and power are the only two things worth grabbing."

Lamar wondered what Carroll was referring to. Deep down he really knew. He paused before speaking and gulped, the knot welling up in his stomach. "Well, the victory certainly feels great."

"From now on, every Sunday you'll be at the stadium, not at church," Rosenbloom said. "It looks like the NFL has a new member of our congregation."

—∞—

In the game's postmortem, Ben Funk of the Associated Press wrote, "Joe Namath is the greatest sports prophet since Cassius Clay called the rounds in which his foes would fall."

—∞—

The AFL had reached parity with the NFL.

CHAPTER FORTY-NINE

One year after that improbable Jets victory, Lamar's Chiefs duplicated the AFL's remarkable accomplishment by dominating the Minnesota Vikings 21–7 in Super Bowl IV. Lamar's vison was now complete. Two years later, the Baltimore Colts held a news conference at a Chesapeake Bay restaurant. They announced that Chicago businessman Robert Irsay had purchased the Los Angeles Rams and then swapped them even up for Carroll Rosenbloom's Baltimore Colts. By trading the Colts for the Rams, Carroll avoided paying $4.5 million in federal taxes.

Seven years after that improbable news conference, the ever-calculating Georgia had learned well from Carroll, her husband and mentor. She decided that the City of Angels would be a considerably livelier town if she lived in it solo. On April 2, 1979, the fateful morning of Carroll's demise, Georgia slid her screen door and let the soft wind blowing from the surrounding palm trees fill her negligee.

She glided out onto her Florida deck, wearing a purple cover-up and carrying her morning coffee. Georgia lit a Parliament and let her eyes slide slowly to the end of the Golden Beach dock, where Carroll swam cadenced laps in the cobalt-colored Atlantic.

Even at seven decades plus, her husband was still handsome and fit, wide in the shoulders and flat in the stomach.

Georgia analyzed Carroll's steady, rhythmic, hypnotic motion as if she was trying to memorize it. She allowed her eyes to shift momentarily from her husband to her Rolex. It was exactly 9 a.m. With that, she stood and retreated into the kitchen where she dumped the remains of her coffee into the sink. She poured a fresh cup and despite the early morning hour diluted the black brew with brandy.

She had barely jammed the cork back into the bottle when Carroll suddenly began splashing, thrashing, and kicking, his face wincing, his aching arms and burning lungs struggling to stay above the surface. With his face flushing, ears pinging, Carroll splashed violently until the water pressure finally broke something inside his head. He felt a razor pain in his chest, like a sharp shard of glass working its way through the tissue of his lungs. He struggled, snorted, and scraped until a strange moment of recognition swam through his mind as though he had seen the entirety of this life reduced to the flip of a coin that had only one outcome. The blue-black water faded away and his vision became ever darker. Finally, all pain stopped. All thoughts stopped. All life stopped.

By the time Georgia returned to the deck, Carroll was gone. She drained her drink and ambled back into the kitchen to call the authorities, her exquisitely manicured fingernails closing the curtain behind her.

From this moment forward, Georgia knew that she would never have some condescending, unfaithful son of a bitch telling her how to dress, how to act, or when she should or shouldn't speak. She was now the owner of one of the NFL's most prestigious teams and one of the most powerful women in the world.

Picking her teddy bear off the bed, she casually tossed it into the trash basket. Georgia wouldn't need that comfort bear — or anything — or anyone else — ever again.

POSTSCRIPT

F ewer than twelve months after Carroll's death, Georgia married her sixth husband, Domenic Frontiere. Predictably, that union also ended in divorce. The most powerful woman in football history then moved the Rams to her hometown of St. Louis in 1995, leaving the nation's second-largest TV market without an NFL franchise for twenty years. The St. Louis Rams would appear in two Super Bowls, winning the title in 1999. Despite the speculation and "mystery" surrounding Carroll's death, Georgia Rosenbloom lived a happy life before dying of breast cancer in 2008 at the age of eighty.

As for Lamar and his now-champion Chiefs? They continued to evolve with Kansas City, becoming one of the NFL's most rabid fan bases, annually drawing more than 70,000 loud supporters into a sold-out Arrowhead Stadium. Lamar's other visions also proved prophetic, as co-founder of Major League Soccer (MLS) and World Championship Tennis (WCT).

Lamar Hunt was voted into the Pro Football Hall of Fame in 1972. In 1985 the AFL championship trophy was renamed the Lamar Hunt Trophy. Lamar was also honored by induction into the National Soccer and International Tennis Halls of Fame.

Lamar Hunt passed away in 2006 at seventy-four years of age. His legacy lives on as the Hunt family, under the direction of Lamar's son, Clark, still owns and runs the Kansas City Chiefs. In 2020 the Chiefs were victorious in Super Bowl LIV with a rousing 31–20 victory over the San Francisco 49ers. Of course, Lamar's wife of forty-two years was in the stands that day. Norma has attended all fifty-four Super Bowls.

—ᘓ—

It entertains us, this business of football.

Football is a game. Professional football is a business. Yes, football is big business, plain and simple. And whenever a large amount of money is thrown around behind closed doors without public scrutiny, corruption is sure to follow.

Billions of dollars are bet on football every season, but it's impossible to fix a game, right?

Maybe, maybe not.

Jimmy "The Weasel" Fratianno claimed he had bought numerous officials for Frank Costello.

In *The Godfather Part II,* when Michael Corleone decides to whack the diminutive Mob boss Hyman Roth (based on Meyer Lansky), Michael says to Tom Hagen, "If history has taught us anything, it's that nothing's impossible, difficult but not impossible." Sure, fixing a pro football game wouldn't be easy, but it's hardly impossible.

An Unauthorized History of Football, a PBS documentary, was the opening episode of *Frontline* and the only one unavailable for public access. The episode outlined a history of the league's gambling problems and detailed alleged associations of owners and players with gamblers and organized crime.

One gambler interviewed, John Piazza, said that a coach, quarterback, and defensive captain of a team that he wouldn't identify had been paid to fix four games in '68, '69, and '70. Jessica Savitch, the host of that controversial 1983 *Frontline,* died shortly after that broadcast in a freak automobile accident. The media reported rumors that Jessica had a cocaine problem; however, the Bucks County Coroner ruled that, at the time of her death, she had no traces of drugs in her system.

—ᘓ—

From a practical matter, without that victory of the underdog New York Jets in '69, the merger could have been a disaster for CBS and NBC. Some of the staunchest NFL fans in Pittsburgh, Baltimore, and Cleveland were up in arms after their teams left for the "weaker" league. After the upset, things quieted down a bit, and a "wait till next year" sentiment began to well up in Baltimore, where the Colts conveniently ended up in the same division with that blasted hippie, Joe Namath.

Nine months after that historic '69 Super Bowl, ABC introduced Monday Night Football. Who played in that first historic game? Joe Namath's New York Jets and Art Modell's Cleveland Browns. Rozelle, Modell, and the networks could not have planned it better. Meanwhile, Art Rooney reinvested the $3 million that he had received to switch to "the weaker league" to build Pittsburgh's championship years of the '70s and their famous "Steel Curtain."

Namath and his teammates' victory secured the two leagues an unimaginable amount of future TV revenue. The game was almost too good to be true. Particularly troubling was the merger of television, football, and then Congress. Television looks at football pragmatically, each game its own unique program script. A Colts slaughter of the Jets would have confirmed the public's suspicion of a gross imbalance between the two leagues.

The merged league that this fairytale is based on has produced unprecedented amounts of income and propelled the billionaires who own those teams to unimaginable wealth and power. When each owner put up $100,000, the group was collectively known as The Foolish Club. The Dallas Cowboys alone are now estimated to be worth $5.5 billion.

Namath wasn't worth $100,000 a year? Largely because of the merger and that historic game played in '69, Chicago Bears backup quarterback Nick Foles, earned $8 million per year, starting in 2020 with a three-year guarantee.

—✺—

Like Congressman Emanuel Celler had warned, with the merger of television and football, wagering on sports increased by 600 percent. Football betting soon became the fastest-growing form of gambling in Las Vegas.

One of Rozelle's successors, Roger Goodell, reveals just how much the league's attitude toward gambling has changed with the times. Last year, the NFL selected Caesars Palace as their official sponsor. Mark Davis, Al's son, has moved his Raiders to a new stadium in Las Vegas this year. "We think sports gambling in many ways creates a lot more engagement for our fans," Goodell said. "It's another opportunity for them to engage with our game." Now ironically, due to the coronavirus pandemic, Davis's Las Vegas Raiders are playing in front of empty stands!

Goodell said that the league aspires to gross revenues of $27 billion by 2027. The stadium recently constructed for the Los Angeles Rams in Inglewood alone cost an estimated $3 billion.

All of this because, at critical junctures, the AFL's Founding Fathers, along with NFL commissioner Pete Rozelle and his pioneering predecessor, Bert Bell, managed to put aside aggressive agendas and personal resentments to forge a business model rooted in competitive parity and a quasi-socialist form of revenue sharing.

Emanuel Celler certainly wouldn't blame the Oakland Raiders for ripping the heart out of their diehard fans to move to Las Vegas, where, despite the city's underfunded schools and medieval roads, Vegas will shell out close to $1 billion for a new stadium.

It's certainly not the league's fault that ESPN will pay them $15.2 billion to broadcast their product until 2021 or that DirecTV will pay them $12 billion till 2022 or that Fox will pay them $9.9 billion till 2022 or that CBS will pay them $9 billion till 2021 or that NBC will pay them $8.55 billion till 2021 or that Verizon will pay them 2.5 billion through 2023

It's not the league's fault that revenue from merchandise, gate receipts, and broadcasting rights will net each team $255 million this year. In the last decade, the price of a Super Bowl ad has increased by 75 percent. A thirty-second spot for advertising in Super Bowl LIV will cost $5 million. The money is deemed well spent. The last eight Super Bowls are the most-watched programs in television history.

—ᴍ—

The contentious relationship between Al Davis and the NFL continued for another forty years with multiple suits and countersuits. In 2007, NFL Films chose this feud as the greatest in NFL history, citing almost half a century of animosity between Brooklyn Al and Pete Rozelle. Many believe that the root of Davis's bitterness was the surreptitious way the NFL-AFL merger was pushed behind his back.

Five years after Davis pulled Lamar aside at Shea Stadium to suggest someone interfere with the Super Bowl outcome, Davis would be involved in a questionable land investment deal involving Teamster pension funds with known gambler and Mob associate Allen Glick. Glick was immortalized in the Martin Scorsese film, Casino, as the thinly disguised Mr. Green (Kevin Pollack), who stood by and allowed Frank "Lefty" Rosenthal (Robert De-Niro as Sam "Ace" Rothstein) and Tony "The Ant" Spilotro (Joe Pesci as Nicky Santoro) to skim millions of dollars off the top of casino profits.

Rosenthal, a sports handicapper, bookie, and sports fixer, was variously billed as Glick's entertainment director, assistant, and food and beverage manager. He allegedly reported to his bosses in Chicago and Kansas City, who had arranged Glick's hotel purchases with $62 million in loans from Jimmy Hoffa's corrupt Teamsters Central States Pension Fund. Spilotro was a hitman for the Mob, responsible at last count for twenty-five murders. His own body would eventually be found next to his brother's in a shallow grave in an Indiana cornfield.

Assuming no personal responsibility for Glick's loan, Davis would buy 25 percent of a $25 million-dollar mall from Glick for

$5,000. Real estate experts told UPI news that it is unusual for a limited partner to receive tax losses of more than six times his investment. In Davis's case, his tax savings equaled 200 times his original $5,000 investment. The investment would produce $2.1 million in Federal tax losses for Davis, which he would use to shelter his personal income.

When Commissioner Pete Rozelle was informed of the "land deal," his response in New York was predictable. "This is an old story," he said. "We have no comment."

Pete Rozelle always made a grand show of publicly fining or reprimanding players but never the owners. In 1969, Rozelle forced Namath to either give up part-ownership in Bachelors III, a Manhattan bar/restaurant, or leave football. Namath tearfully gave up football but soon changed his mind. Namath said he didn't even know that people with questionable characters frequented his place.

Yet Eagles owner Leonard Tose had admitted to losing $2.5 million in gambling casinos in Las Vegas and Atlantic City. Eddie DeBartolo was turned down by Bowie Kuhn four times when attempting to buy a baseball team because of ties to the underworld but was allowed to buy the 49ers. Al Davis got a $100,000 finder's fee.

Rozelle said and did nothing.

According to the American Gaming Association, an estimated $150 billion a year is wagered illegally on college and pro football.

Bear in mind, it would be impossible for bookies to operate if the media didn't obligingly print or report point spreads, injury reports, and game conditions. Football, gambling, and television are so entangled that the games on the coast have been moved from 4 p.m. EST. to 4:25 p.m.—to accommodate the networks, yes—but to accommodate the bookies too. Gamblers don't want to bet the late games until they know how much they've lost or won betting the earlier ones. Despite all the aforementioned—professional football's sordid past and the amount of money funneled to the Mob through illegal gambling—America turns a blind eye.

ABOUT THE AUTHORS

In **Billy O'Connor**'s colorful life, the Irish immigrant was a Vietnam vet, a Teamster, a bookie, a bar owner, and an alcoholic and drug user. He also served twenty years with the New York City Fire Department and was a first responder at Ground Zero. The tragedy of 9/11 spurred the morally rudderless FDNY lieutenant to have a moment of clarity. At the age of sixty-two, he put the plug in  the jug and enrolled at the University of Florida. After earning his BA in journalism, he now writes and performs stand-up comedy full-time.

This current book about gambling and the NFL is Billy O'Connor's fourth and his second with Frank Pace. He co-wrote *If These Lips Could Talk* with the prolific producer. O'Connor's first novel, *Confessions of a Bronx Bookie*, was autobiographical.

Frank Pace is a prolific television producer and author. His more than 700 network credits include *Murphy Brown, Suddenly Susan, Head of the Class,* and *George Lopez*. Frank has also produced four movies including the Emmy Award winning, *Babe Ruth*. This is his second book with Billy O'Connor, having co-written *If These Lips Could Talk* with Billy. He also co-wrote two books with  *New York Times* best-selling author Armen Keteyian: *Rod Carew's Art and Science of Hitting* (Viking/Penguin) and *Rod Carew's Hit to Win* (Minnesota Press). Pace worked in the long-defunct World Football League for two years and was on the field the day Marty Schottenheimer retired as a player during the morning session and returned as the linebacker coach after lunch. Marty would become the eighth-winningest coach in the NFL.

INDEX

A

Aaron, Hank 183
ABC 74-77, 117-118, 120, 122, 208
Adams, Bud 26-27, 30-31, 39, 41, 43-44, 58, 60, 62, 64-65, 83-85, 89, 94-95, 98, 149, 174-175
Adderley, Herb 176
Alabama Crimson Tide 131
Alcindor, Lew 128
Ali, Muhammad 127-128, 177, 181
Ameche, Alan 17-18
American Football League (AFL) 61-62, 67-68, 76, 78, 83, 89, 92, 95, 102, 104, 108-109, 117, 121-122, 129, 134, 136-137, 142, 146-148, 150, 163, 166, 175-176, 184, 186-187, 189, 197, 200, 203, 206
American Football League Hall of Fame 98
American Gaming Association 211
Arrowhead Stadium 96-97, 206

B

Bachelors III 211
Baltimore Colts 7, 13-19, 22, 32, 37, 48, 63, 86, 98, 110, 118, 182, 192-194, 196-202, 204, 208
Baltimore Herald 85
Baltimore Sun 86, 182
Barber, Stew 84
Bartle, H. Roe 96
Bell, Bert 43, 47-50, 52-53, 58, 66, 101, 209
Belmont Park, New York 87
Bench, Johnny 183
Berry, Raymond 16, 23, 63
Besselink, Al 15
Beverly, Randy 198
Bidwell, Bill and Charles 26
Blanda, George 83, 89
Blue Ridge Overalls 23
Boggs, Hale 170, 172-173
Borman, Frank 140
Boston, Massachusetts 26-27, 39, 68
Boston Patriots 83
Bowman, Steve 131
Brasi, Luca 87
Brock, Cathy 7
Brock, Tom 7
Brodie, John 15, 161-162
Brooklyn Dodgers 39, 96
Brown, Jim 17, 128
Bryant, Bear 129-131
Buchanan, Buck 161
Buffalo Bills 84, 152, 158
Buffalo, New York 39, 68

C

Caesars Palace 209
Campanella, Roy 39
Capone, Al 71
Carew, Rod 183
Carlos, John 128
Carson, Johnny 117
CBS 67, 112, 118, 120-121, 171, 174, 180, 208-209
Celler, Emanuel 49, 52-53, 172, 209
Chandler, Don 176
Chavez, Cesar 180
Chesapeake Bay Restaurant 204
Chesler, Lou 17, 32-33, 35, 37-38, 70, 196
Chicago Bears 26, 71, 162, 208
Chicago Cardinals 25-26, 30
Chicago, Illinois 25-26
Civil Rights Act 115, 179
Clams, Johnny 7
Clay, Cassius 127, 203
Clemente, Roberto 183
Cleveland Browns 22, 196, 208
Conerly, Charlie 16
Cooke, Sam 128
Coppola, Mike 70
Cosell, Howard 104, 106, 134-135, 141, 162, 177
Costello, Frank 108, 207
Cotton Bowl 74
Cowboys 92, 95, 146
Cronkite, Walter 112, 139
Crosby, Bing 107
Crow, Jim 115

D

Dallas Cowboys 72, 75, 145, 175, 208
Dallas Observer 13
Dallas Texans 92, 95
Dallas, Texas 25, 27-28, 39, 51, 59, 62-63, 68, 72, 79, 85, 96, 109, 112-113, 146, 168
Davis, Al 99, 136-137, 146, 148, 158-159, 161-163, 188-191, 209-211
Davis, Mark 209
Dawson, Lenny 95-96
Dean, Dizzy 183
DeBartolo, Eddie 211
Dempsey, Jack 107
DeNiro, Robert 210
Denver Broncos 83
Denver, Colorado 26-27, 39, 42, 68
DeRogatis, Al 197-199, 202
Detroit Tigers 183
Diamond, Neil 136
Diem, President Ngo Din 139
DiMaggio, Joe 103, 126
Dirksen, Everett 35-37, 102, 168, 170, 172-173

D (cont.)

Ditka, Mike 161, 162
Drysdale, Don 183

E

Ebbets Field 39
Eisenhower, Dwight 90-91
Erasmus Hall High School 136
Ewbank, Weeb 19, 110, 126, 193, 202

F

Fawcett, Farrah 182
Fischer, Bobby 136
Five O'clock Club 108
Flores, Tom 83
Flushing Meadows Park 109
Foles, Nick 208
Foolish Club, The 39, 42, 78-79, 89-90, 93, 98, 117, 124, 208
Ford, Gerald 102
Foss, Joe 60, 73, 78, 93, 98, 102, 121-122, 137, 142, 146
Fratianno, Jimmy (The Weasel) 207
Fresno, California 118
Frontiere, Domenic 206
Frontiere, Georgia 99
Funk, Ben 203

G

Gabriel, Roman 161
Gambino, Carlos 86
Gaye, Marvin 128
General Development 70
Giancana, Sam 113
Gibson, Bob 183
Gillman, Sid 83
Gleason, Jackie 20, 133
Glick, Allen 210
Gogolak, Pete 158-159, 162
Goldwater, Barry 179
Goodell, Roger 209
Gowdy, Curt 186, 197-202
Grange, Red 126
Green Bay Packers 174-176
Grier, Roosevelt 181
Gummere, Richard 99

H

Haddad, Mitchell 99
Hagen, Tom 207
Halas, George 26, 71
Hamill, Pete 107
Haynes, Abner 89, 95
Herz, Alice 138
Hess, Leon 109, 126
Hicks, Dwight 7
Hill, Jerry 199
Hilton, Barron 39, 41, 43, 69, 79-80, 89, 93-95, 98, 142-143
Hodges, Gil 39
Hoffa, Jimmy 108
Hoover, J. Edgar 167

Hope, Bob 117
Hornung, Paul 105-106
Houston Oilers 89, 95, 140, 162, 175
Houston, Texas 26-27, 30, 39, 62, 68, 85, 137, 149
Howsam, Bob 26-27, 39, 42
Hudson, Jim 199
Huff, Sam 17
Humphry, Hubert 181
Hunt, Clark 206
Hunter, Catfish 183
Hunt, H.L. 13, 39, 45, 52, 69, 80, 97, 113, 122-123, 152, 194, 202
Hunt, Jr., Lamar 28-29, 184
Hunt, Lamar 13-14, 19, 23-24, 26-31, 39, 41, 43-45, 51, 58-62, 64, 69, 73, 75-80, 83, 85, 89-90, 93-98, 108, 117, 122, 124, 129-130, 132, 134, 138, 142-147, 149, 151-153, 158-159, 164, 167-168, 174-175, 184, 188-190, 200-204, 206
Hunt, Norma 124, 151, 153, 174, 207
Hunt, Rosemary 25, 28, 45-46, 59, 63, 95-96

I
Ice Bowl 175
Inglewood, California 209
International Tennis Hall of Fame 206
Irsay, Robert 204
Iselin, Phil 109, 126

J
Jackson, Reggie 183
Jamaica Race Track 100
Jeppesen Field 89
Jet Stream (magazine) 103
Johansson, Ingemar 127
Johnson Lyndon (LBJ) 102, 112, 115-116, 138-139, 168, 173, 179, 181

K
Kansas City Chiefs 96-97, 123, 135, 174-175, 204, 206
Kansas City, Missouri 95-96, 206
Karras, Alex 105-106
Kemp, Jack 89
Kennedy, Bobby 36-37, 116, 167, 178
Kennedy, Jacqueline 98
Kennedy, John F. (Jack) 33-34, 37, 90, 98, 112-113, 178
Kennedy, Joseph (Joe) 33-37, 90, 113, 167-168
Kennedy, Robert 179-181
Keteyian, Armen 7, 213
Khrushchev, Nikita 90
King, Martin Luther 114, 138, 179-180

Klosterman, Don 159, 161-162
Kuhn, Bowie 211
Kunz, Carl 98

L
Lafayette Park 101
Lamar Hunt Trophy 206
Lamonica, Daryle 175, 186-187
Lansky, Meyer 32, 70, 207
Larson, Don 183
Las Vegas, Nevada 209
Las Vegas Raiders 209
LeBaron, Eddie 95
Lee, Peggy 20
Leffler, Warren K. 101
Lincoln Memorial 114
Lindeman, Carl 120-121
Lombardi, Vince 73, 106, 154, 175-176
Longhorn Country Club 124
Long, Huey 173
Long, Russell 172-173
Lord, Julia 7
Los Angeles, California 15, 19, 39-40, 94
Los Angeles Chargers 89, 136
Los Angeles Coliseum 141, 174
Los Angeles Rams 22, 66-67, 72, 161, 204, 206, 209
Los Angeles Times 194
Louis, Joe 127
Louisville, Kentucky 68
Love Field 146
Lucia Pamela and her Musical Pirates 56

M
Major League Soccer (MLS) 206
Malcolm X 127
Mantle, Mickey 103, 107, 183
Mara, Tim 48, 50, 100, 153
Mara, Wellington 145, 149-150, 158, 161-163
Marcello, Carlos 173
Marciano, Rocky 103, 127
Marshall, George 101
Martin, Dean 133
Matte, Tom 183, 199, 201
Mays, Willie 108, 183
McCarthy, Eugene 179-180
McCarthy, Joe 178
McClain, Denny 183
McKinley, President 113
McLaney, Mike 17, 70-71
McLuhan, Marshall 36, 88
McNamara, Robert 116, 139
McPhail, Bill 120, 171
Mecom, Jr., John 173
Mecom, Sr., John 173
Memphis, Tennessee 114, 179
Meredith, Don 72, 74-75
Miami, Florida 32, 68
Miami Herald 194
Miami Touchdown Club 194
Michaels, Lou 182-183, 197
Minneapolis, Minnesota 26, 39, 68

Minnesota Vikings 204
Mitchell, Tom 198
Modell, Art 22-23, 48-49, 68, 71, 86, 105, 121, 132, 145, 165, 189, 201, 208
Modell, Jennifer 132
Modell, Patricia 132
Monday Night Football 208
Monmouth Racetrack 109
Monte Carlo Casino 32
Moore, Charlie 7
Moore, Erin 7
Moore, Frankie 7
Moore, Thomas 76-77
Moore, Tom 117
Morrall, Earl 182, 192-193, 196-201
Moses, Robert 40-41
Murchison, Clint 72, 145, 190
Murder Incorporated 32
Music Corporation of America (MCA) 107
Mutscheller, Jim 18
My Lai Massacre 113
Myra, Steve 15

N
Namath, Joe 103, 126, 129-133, 135, 141-142, 163, 182, 186-188, 192-194, 197, 200-201, 203, 208, 211
National Football League (NFL) 14-15, 26, 31, 41-44, 52-53, 62, 65, 68-72, 75-76, 78, 80, 83, 85-86, 93, 96, 101, 105, 109, 117, 120-121, 125, 130, 135-137, 140, 146-147, 149-151, 153, 158-159, 161-163, 170-171, 173, 175, 185, 189, 190, 197, 200, 203, 206, 208-210
National Soccer Hall of Fame 206
NBC 18, 107, 120-122, 174, 187, 208-209
Newcombe, Don 39
New Orleans, Louisiana 68
New Orleans Saints 173
New York City, New City 103
New York Daily News 194
New York Giants 7, 13-14, 15-18, 40, 42, 96, 100, 109, 135, 149, 158, 160, 162
New York Jets 7, 109-111, 126, 134-135, 150, 163, 182, 186-187, 191-194, 196-199, 201-202, 204, 208
New York Knicks 75
New York Mets 109
New York Titans 92-94, 104, 107-109, 135
New York Yankees 39
NFL Films 210
Nickerson Field 83
Nixon, Richard 91, 181
Nobis, Tommy 140
North Vietnam 116, 138

O

Oakland, California 176, 186-187
Oakland Raiders 99, 136-137,
  146, 150, 175, 187, 191, 209
O'Brien, Davey 43-44, 47, 51
O'Connor, Billy 212-213
O'Connor, Jennifer 7
O'Donnell, Kenny 91
O'Malley, Walter 39-41
Orange Bowl 129-130, 175
Orr, Jimmy 199

P

Pace, Frank 212-213
Pace, Karen 7
Pamela, Georgia 32, 56-57, 67,
  87-88, 112, 118-119, 144-145,
  155-157
Pamela, Lucia 119
Parilli, Babe 83, 193
Peale, Norman Vincent 185
Pentagon Papers 113
Pesci, Joe 210
Piazza, John 207
Pittsburgh, Pennsylvania 63
Pollack, Kevin 210
Polo Grounds 40, 92, 108, 135
Poor People's March 101
Porter, Ron 198
Preston Marshall, George 85
Pro Football Hall of Fame 206

Q

Queens, New York 110

R

Rash, Shirley 7
Reese, Pee Wee 39
Richardson, Willie 197-198
Ringo, Jim 73
Robbie, Joe 142
Robinson, Jackie 39
Rooney, Art 23, 48, 50, 71, 105,
  153, 160, 165, 189, 201, 208
Rosenbloom, Carroll 17, 22-23,
  26, 32, 34-38, 48-50, 54-55,
  57, 63-67, 70, 72, 85-88,
  95, 98, 105, 112-113, 120,
  145, 147, 150, 153, 155-156,
  162, 164-169, 173, 176, 183,
  188-189, 191, 197-198, 200,
  202-204
Rosenbloom, Georgia (Mrs.
  Carroll) 99, 164-166,
  197-198, 204-206
Rosenthal, Frank (Lefty) 210
Rote, Kyle 197-199
Rowe, Abbie 98
Royal, Darryl 131
Rozelle, Pete 66-68, 80, 86-87,
  102, 105-106, 120-121,
  144-145, 148-150, 152,
  162-163, 165, 170-173, 176,
  184-185, 196, 198, 208-211

Russell, Bill 75, 128
Russell, Richard 115
Ruth, Babe 107
Ryan, Bob 147
Ryan, Tommy 191

S

Saban, Lou 83
Sample, Johnny 198
San Diego, California 93, 95
San Francisco 49ers 149, 162,
  206
San Francisco, California 40
Sauer, George 198-199
Savitch, Jessica 207
Schenkel, Chris 15-18
Scherick, Edgar 76-77, 117
Schottenheimer, Marty 213
Schram, Hank 174
Schramm, Tex 23-24, 30, 72,
  75, 145-147, 151
Scorsese, Martin 210
Scott, Ray 176
Seaver, Tom 183
Seven Arts Ltd. (Seven Arts
  Productions) 23, 70
Shaw, Billy 84
Shea Stadium 109, 134-135,
  188, 203, 210
Shor, Toots 103
Shula, Coach 193
Shula, Don 199-201
Siegel, Bugsy 32
Simpson, Jim 130
Sinatra, Frank 20, 103, 107,
  108, 117, 142
Sioux Falls, South Dakota 61
Sirhan, Sirhan 181
Smith, Charlie 187
Smith, Tommie 128
Snell, Matt 198
Snider, Duke 39
Soda, Charlie 79
Southeast Asia 90, 139
South Vietnam 139
Spadia, Lou 145, 149, 162
Spilotro, Tony (The Ant) 210
Sports Illustrated 137
Starr, Bart 175-176
Stephenson, Adlai 91
St. Louis Cardinals 130
St. Louis, Missouri 206
St. Louis Rams 206
Stoneham, Horace 40-41
Stram, Hank 83
Streisand, Barbra 136
Sullivan, Bill 98
Sullivan, Billy 26-27, 31, 39
Summit Hotel 188
Super Bowl 185, 187-188
Super Bowl III 7, 192
Super Bowl IV 204
Super Bowl LIV 11, 206, 210

T

Taylor, Elizabeth 117
Taylor, Otis 136
Teamsters Central States
  Pension Fund 210
Tet Offensive 139
Texas 83-84
Texas Longhorns 83-84,
  130-131
Texas Tech 83
Thompson, Chuck 15-16, 18
Timoney, John 187-188, 191
Toots Shor's 107-108, 126, 133
Tose, Leonard 211
Truman, Harry 101
Turner, Jim 198, 201

U

Unitas, Dorothy 132
Unitas, Johnny 16, 18-19, 23,
  132, 193, 196-197, 201
Universal Controls 70
US Civilian Conservation Corps
  23
USS Maddox 139

V

Valley, Wayne 79, 98, 137
Vietnam 91, 179
Vietnam War 113, 115, 186
View Inn 152

W

Warhol, Andy 36-37
War Memorial Stadium 84
Warren Commission 113
Warren, Earl 108
Washington, D.C. 52, 101
Washington Post 106
Washington Redskins 85,
  101-102
Wellington, Mara 160
Werblin, Sonny 107-110, 118,
  126, 129-130, 132-134, 136,
  182, 202
Wilkinson, Bud 130
Williams, Edward Bennett 102
Wilson, Ralph 39, 42, 89, 93,
  98, 152-153, 158-159, 200
Winter, Max 26-27, 39, 42, 69,
  70, 79
Wismer, Harry 39, 41-42, 69,
  74, 76-77, 82, 92-95, 98, 104,
  108, 189
Wolfner, Walter 25-27
Wood, Willie 174
World Championship Tennis
  (WCT) 206
World's Fair 109

Y

Yankee Stadium 15

Other Books by
FRANK PACE AND BILLY O'CONNOR

Combustible
A Fireman's Road to Hell Hits a Detour at 9/11
By Billy O'Connor and Frank Pace

Book Excerpt – Chapter 1

On this last morning of the first year of the new century, the sun was trying to crash through the thick clouds blanketing the South Bronx. Inside the five Boroughs' busiest firehouse, Conor Kilcullen was sipping his coffee when three air-horn blasts shattered the silence. The house-watchman's voice thundered over the intercom: "Everybody goes, truck, engine, and chief. Everybody goes. Get out. Get out. Get out!"

(Dissolve to later in the chapter)

…Conor's flashlight lit a foggy, soft glow into the shadows. His left hand dragged the wooden hook and the heavy, steel Halligan tool, while his right hand splayed the floor for balance, his elbows inching ahead of his knees, the little muscles in his hands and thighs twitching and dripping sweat.

Conor's stomach seemed to be jarred loose, his heart rattling inside his ribs. The eerie silence made him think his ears had failed him until he heard the measured sounds of his own breathing. Then out of the tomb-like silence, he perceived a voice almost like an open-mouthed statue laughing at his recklessness. No sound, just a voice taunting him that he had overplayed his hand.

He inched farther and farther, absolutely convinced he was about to die until he stumbled upon a miracle. The tip of his nose almost smacked into a small, metal wheel. A wooden leg seemed to climb from it.

Was he lucky enough to have found a crib?

Shimmying the wood, his gloved hand probed between the slats and felt a bump in the bedding. He stood, held his breath, and lifted his face-piece.

It was an infant. Two questions now remained—did the baby still have a heartbeat and, if so, could they get out alive?

Available Fall 2021

If These Lips Could Talk

By Frank Pace with Billy O'Connor

From the edge of Hollywood's spotlight and right into the locker rooms of America, *If These Lips Could Talk* gives you a producer's unfettered access to big-named actors and athletes you have known and admired through the years. Be warned, some of these people are not who they appear to be.

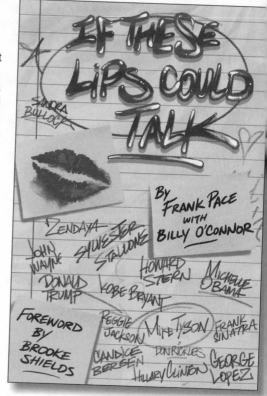

Imagine you are at the Emmy's with Candice Bergen, or with Sandra Bullock at the world premiere of *Oceans 8*, or that you have written Rod Carew's Baseball Hall of Fame induction speech. Now imagine you are seated on a private jet alongside Brooke Shields. One week you are backstage in Sinatra's dressing room with your pal Don Rickles, the next you are taking the first American TV show to the USSR, and all the while you are coaching a girls' high school soccer team to a number one spot in the national rankings.

It is a dream, right?

Now imagine a kid who was hustling nickel tips on a paper route at ten years old, a teenage caddy hanging out with a future mafia kingpin, a mediocre student at a small Valhalla, New York high school going nowhere fast.

Things happened that turned his dream into reality.

If These Lips Could Talk is an exhilarating, breezy, unvarnished peek at what goes on at the edge of the spotlight. This book's not about Frank Pace but about the people he met along the way-a witty, poignant, page-turner that will make you laugh, shake your head and sometimes flat out break your heart.

6x9, 256 pages, $24.95
ISBN: 978-1-948901-63-5

Excerpts from *If These Lips Could Talk...*

BROOKE SHIELDS

The first thing one noticed about Brooke Shields was that despite the beauty she displayed on film and television, no camera had ever done her justice. She was an example of nature perfecting itself, yet she would fearlessly wrestle Hulk Hogan and would think noting of taking a pie in the face. In short, anything for a laugh.

Reggie Jackson was what I expected. He looked me up and down and said, "Do you own a suit?"

"Yes, sir," I said.

"Do you own a tie?"

"Yes, sir," I repeated.

"Do you own a briefcase?"

Again, I said, "Yes."

REGGIE JACKSON

"Good. Come back to the stadium tomorrow. Put on your suit. Wear your tie and bring that briefcase—even if it's empty. We'll sign all these motherfuckers."

That day led to a 40 year association with Rod Carew.

GEORGE LOPEZ

Deb Oppenheimer, an executive producer, stuck her 2 cents in by saying she thought the kitchen didn't look "Mexican enough". I could see George Lopez seethe. "Should we put some jalapenos around the door? Wait until you put the damn Mexicans in it," he bellowed. "Then it will look Mexican."

The kitchen stayed unchanged.

"Donald Trump's office, may I help you?" his secretary asked.

"Mr. Trump, please," I said.

"I am sorry. He's not available."

"Can you tell him that Frank Pace called. I am the producer of Suddenly Susan, and we would like him to appear in an episode."

"Can you hold on, please?"

"Hello, Frank," the man said. "This is Donald Trump. What can I do for you?"

DONALD TRUMP
ON *SUDDENLY SUSAN*

FRANK SINATRA

The moment Sinatra entered the stage, we started rolling. Frank was shown his mark and bellowed, "Where's Rickels?"

Don dashed in from offstage.

"You're wearing a tie for this bit?" Frank asked.

"Frank, please," Don said. "Don't embarrass yourself. Just stand there. Do the line and hope someone remembers who the hell you are."

MORE SPORTS BOOKS
PUBLISHED BY ACCLAIM PRESS

Here Comes the A-Train!
The Story of Basketball Legend Artis Gilmore

By Artis Gilmore with Mark Bruner and Reid Griffith Fontaine

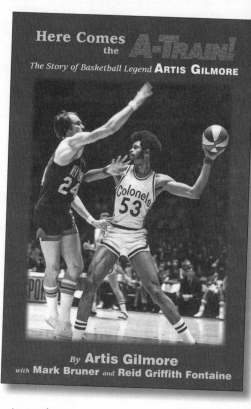

In *Here Comes The A-Train!*, basketball legend Artis Gilmore takes a deep, introspective look at the important life lessons that took him from his rural Florida upbringings to the pinnacle of success in professional basketball. Dubbed "The A-Train" in comparison to the Chicago transit line, there was a time when Artis ruled the game...when protecting the rim and grabbing rebounds were taken for granted. Anyone who drove the lane against the A-Train paid a price. A gentle giant?...opposing teams would disagree!

Named Rookie of the Year, ABA Champion with the Kentucky Colonels, 11-time All-Star, and member of the Naismith Memorial Basketball Hall of Fame (2011), Artis knows that true success in life is not about wins and losses but learning that mastering the small things and overcoming difficult moments are the true keys to greatness.

Artis also looks back at highs and lows of his basketball career, from Carver High School, Jacksonville University, the Kentucky Colonels, and his days in the NBA, including an inside look at other legends of the game throughout his 18-year career.

Here Comes the A-Train! is the perfect gift for any basketball fan and provides sound advice for success in all walks of life.

6x9, 176 pages, $21.95
ISBN: 978-1-942613-90-9

Kentucky Colonels of the American Basketball Association

The Real Story of a Team Left Behind

By Gary P. West with Lloyd "Pink" Gardner

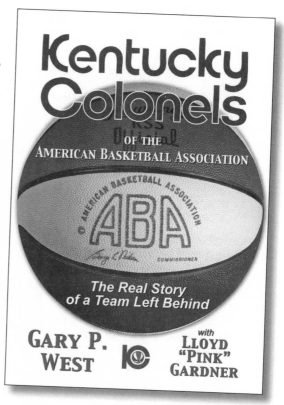

Kentucky Colonels of the American Basketball Association: The Real Story of a Team Left Behind gives an inside look at one of the most intriguing times in the history of professional basketball; and the city of Louisville and the state of Kentucky were enjoying every bit of it.

And then as quickly as the Colonels appeared, they were gone. They had been around just long enough to win a world championship and showcase not only some of the best basketball players in the history of the game, but also some of its most colorful characters.

Perhaps this book should have been written years ago, but there always seemed to be plenty of time. And then one day, a generation or two removed, someone asked what happened to that pro-basketball team back in the '60s and '70s?

BAM, it hits you. This book had to be written.

Here are never-before-told stories that only Lloyd "Pink" Gardner would know. He lived it and Gary P. West wrote it.

A story of colorful owners with family connections to the Lindbergh kidnapping and Hope Diamond; sports agents who would do anything to sign players; a double murder and suicide; a businessman who thought he could do in basketball what he had done with Kentucky Fried Chicken; an insignificant T.V. deal that turned into hundreds of millions of dollars; a team that drafted a 5'6", 55-year-old college professor; and through it all still won a world championship.

6x9, 352 pages, $29.95
ISBN: 978-1-935001-82-9

Better Than Gold
Olympian Kenny Davis and the Most Controversial Basketball Game in History
By Gary West with Kenny Davis

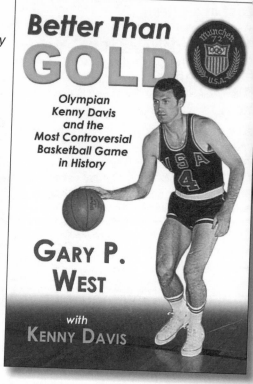

Throughout Kentucky, many thought basketball was as close to heaven as you could get and still be on earth. And the great round ball temple that cast a giant shadow when it came to popularity and influence was in Lexington, Kentucky. That shadow extended all the way to Wayne County.

The Kentucky Wildcats were the young men many throughout the state worshipped, and they felt if you were a really good basketball player you would play for Adolph Rupp.

Kenny Davis didn't go to the University of Kentucky …couldn't play for the Wildcats. And though he only stayed 10 weeks, he did go to Western Kentucky. But then on his way to enrolling at the Air Force Academy, something strange happened. He stopped off at Georgetown College, planning only to stay there for a semester, perhaps not even playing basketball.

Suddenly, out of nowhere, his life changed.

Three college All-American years later, against all odds, Kenny had played in the World Games, Pan American Games, playing the game he learned in Wayne County on five continents. Heady stuff for a boy who had never traveled outside of Kentucky until he went to college.

But the best was yet to come.

The crowning achievement of any American athlete would be to become an Olympian. More often than not it can define one's life. To play basketball on the world's largest stage had become a dream come true, but in the big picture of life's progression, it was no more important than when he became a Wayne County Cardinal.

Basketball became insignificant, however, when a group of terrorist slipped into Munich's Olympic Village and murdered eleven Israeli athletes, thus changing the Olympic world (1972). Suddenly the game Kenny had played all of his life didn't seem as important as it once did. Kenny got to come home… they didn't.

The powers to be, and rightly so, declared that anything less than continuing the Games would be giving into the terrorists.

With all eyes watching, the Americans played the Russians in what became the most controversial ending to a basketball game in history. This game helped to define who Kenny became, and he didn't score a point. Those twelve silver medals Kenny and his teammates refused to accept are today locked in a room in the Olympic Museum in Lausanne, Switzerland.

It's all in these pages, including how Kenny sold millions of tennis shoes during a forty-year career with Converse shoes.

6x9, 304 pages, $26.95
ISBN: 978-1-938905-68-1

Last of a BReed

*A Legendary Kentucky Writer's Journey
Through Six Decades of Sports and
Journalism*

By Billy Reed

Foreword by David Kindred

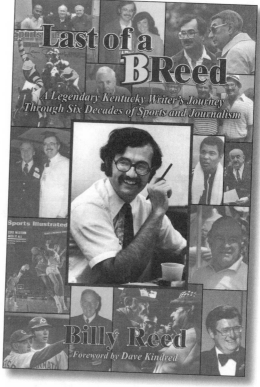

In *Last of a BReed*, award-winning journalist Billy Reed shares a behind-the-scenes look at his career in sports writing, nearly six decades in the making.

One of the most accomplished journalists in Kentucky's history, Billy thrived during the golden era of sports writing, when the *Louisville Courier-Journal* published four editions every night before the internet changed the world.

From his first job as Henry Clay High School beat reporter for the *Lexington Herald-Leader* in 1959, Billy covered all the major sporting events — the World Series, Super Bowl, NCAA Final Four, Triple Crown races, major golf tournaments, and big college football games — and developed personal relationships with the biggest sports personalities — Muhammad Ali, Bob Knight, and Adolph Rupp, to name a few.

Last of a Breed provides a personal reflection on Billy's life as a self-proclaimed "ink-stained wretch" and a tribute to his mentors and colleagues who helped him along the way. Through the years, Billy's clever prose helped fuel the passions of spectators, coaches, players, and trainers alike, and this book gives insight into the craft of developing relationships and creating the stories that defined a generation of athletes.

6x9, 240 pages, $26.95
ISBN: 978-1-948901-00-0

See More Great Books
at
WWW.ACCLAIMPRESS.COM